The Garden of England

The Garden of England

The Counties of Kent, Surrey and Sussex

Text by Robin Whiteman
Photography by Rob Talbot

A Seven Dials Paperback

Text and photographs © Talbot & Whiteman 1995

First published in the United Kingdom in 1995 by
George Weidenfeld & Nicolson

This paperback edition first published in 2003 by
Seven Dials, Weidenfeld & Nicolson
Wellington House, 125 Strand
London, WC2R 0BB

Distributed in the United States of America by
Sterling Publishing Co., Inc.
387 Park Avenue South,
New York, NY 10016-8810

A CIP catalogue record for this book is available from the British Library.

ISBN 1-84188-218-6

Edited by Colin Grant
Designed by Andrew Shoolbred
Map by Bob Monks

HALF-TITLE PAGE: *Old Canonry, Wingham, Kent.* Once a wealthy manor owned by the Archbishops of
Canterbury, Wingham was a favourite resting-place for important personages *en route* from Canterbury
to Cinque Port of Sandwich. A college of secular canons was founded at Wingham in 1282 by Archbishop
John Peckham. The Old Canonry, dated 1286, forms part of a row of timber framed houses that were part
of the college.

FRONTISPIECE: *Bodiam Castle, East Sussex.* In 1385, fearing a French invasion up the estuary of the River
Rother, which was navigable as far as his manor of Bodiam, Sir Edward Dalyngrigge began to build a
rectangular, moated castle with drum towers at each corner and a massive gateway in the centre of the north
side. As well as being a military stronghold, the castle was also designed as a comfortable private residence.
Although the castle was never besieged, the interior was demolished during the Civil War, and in 1916 the
ruins were purchased by George Nathaniel Curzon (first Marquis Curzon of Kedleston), who restored the
exterior and bequeathed, in his own words, 'the most fairy of English castles to the National Trust.

CONTENTS

ACKNOWLEDGEMENTS

Robin Whiteman and Rob Talbot would particularly like to acknowledge the generous cooperation of English Heritage (Historic Properties South-East) and the two National Trust Regional Offices of Kent & East Sussex and Southern for allowing them to take photographs of their properties and sites featured in this book. Additional thanks go to Diana Lanham, Manager of the National Trust Photographic Library. They are also extremely grateful to: Christopher Zeuner, Director, Weald and Downland Open Air Museum; The Sussex Archaeological Society for permission to take photographs at the Roman Palace (Fishbourne), the Priest House (West Hoathly), Michelham Priory and Lewes Castle; the Royal Horticultural Society, Wisley; Museum of Kent Life, Cobtree; Quentin and Christopher Lloyd at Great Dixter; Robin Loder of Leonardslee Gardens; Mr and Mrs John Warde of Squerryes Court; Leeds Castle Enterprises Ltd; Hever Castle (near Edenbridge); Mother Concordia Scott and the Trustees of Minster Abbey; Philip G.L. Case for access to St John's Church, Wotton; and Mrs Glenys B. Putland, Treasurer, Eastbourne Heritage Centre. Special thanks go to Judith Dooling. Appreciation also goes to all those individuals and organizations too numerous to mention by name who nevertheless have made such a valuable contribution.

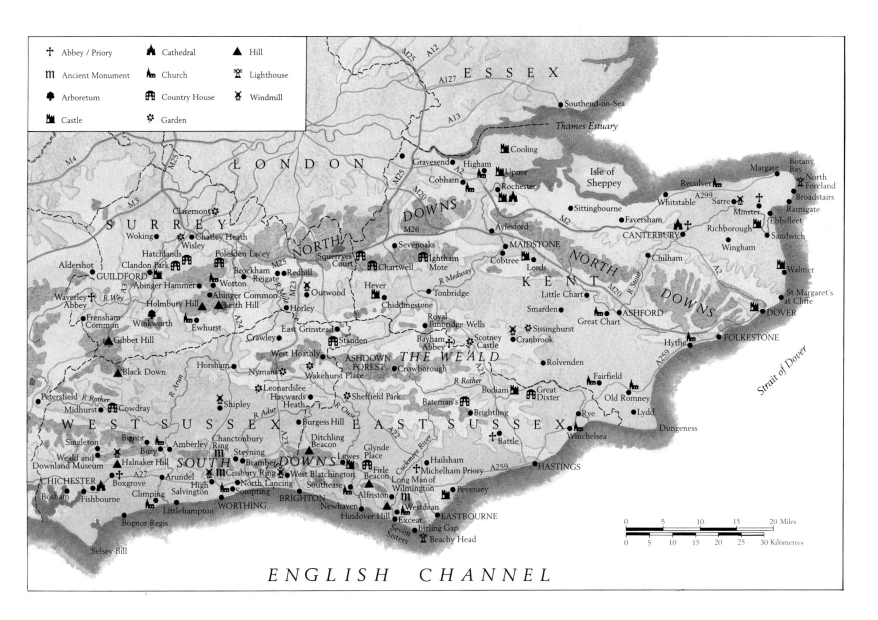

Legend

✝ Abbey / Priory   ♜ Cathedral   ▲ Hill

ⰾ Ancient Monument   ♙ Church   ⚒ Lighthouse

♣ Arboretum   ⌂ Country House   ✴ Windmill

♜ Castle   ✾ Garden

ESSEX

LONDON

SURREY

Southend-on-Sea

Thames Estuary

Cooling

Gravesend   Higham   Upnor   Isle of Sheppey   Margate   Botany Bay

Cobham   Rochester   North Foreland

Reculver   Broadstairs

Sittingbourne   Whitstable   Sarre   Minster   Ramsgate

Faversham   Ebbsfleet

CANTERBURY   Richborough   Sandwich

Claremont

Woking   Chatley Heath   Wisley

Hatchlands   Polesden Lacey

Aldershot   Clandon Park

GUILDFORD   Brockham   Reigate   Redhill

Abinger Hammer   Wotton

Sevenoaks   Squerryes Court   Chartwell   Ightham Mote

MAIDSTONE   Cobtree   Leeds

NORTH DOWNS

KENT

Aylesford   Chilham

Wingham

Waverley Abbey   R Wey   Abinger Common   Leith Hill

Holmbury Hill

Frensham Common   Winkworth   Ewhurst

Hever   Tonbridge   Little Chart

Chiddingstone   Smarden   Great Chart   ASHFORD

Walmer

St Margaret's at Cliffe

DOVER

Gibbet Hill

Black Down

Horley   East Grinstead   Standen   Royal Tunbridge Wells   Bayham Abbey   Scotney Castle   Cranbrook   Sissinghurst

Crawley   West Hoathly

Horsham   Nymans   Wakehurst Place   ASHDOWN FOREST   THE WEALD   Crowborough

FOLKESTONE   Hythe

Strait of Dover

Rolvenden   Fairfield   Bodiam   Great Dixter   Old Romney

R Rother

Petersfield   R Rother   Leonardslee   Haywards Heath   Sheffield Park   Bateman's   Brightling   Rye   Lydd

Midhurst   Cowdray   Shipley

WEST SUSSEX   Burgess Hill   EAST SUSSEX   Winchelsea   Dungeness

Singleton   Bignor   Bury   Amberley   Chanctonbury Ring   Ditchling Beacon   Glynde Place   Hailsham   Battle   HASTINGS

Weald and Downland Museum   Halnaker Hill   Steyning   Bramber   SOUTH DOWNS   Lewes   Michelham Priory

CHICHESTER   Boxgrove   Arundel   Cissbury Ring   West Blatchington   Firle Beacon   Long Man of Wilmington   Pevensey

Bosham   Fishbourne   Climping   High Salvington   North Lancing   Sompting   Southease   Alfriston   Westdean   EASTBOURNE

Littlehampton   WORTHING   BRIGHTON   Newhaven   Hindover Hill   Exceat   Seven Sisters   Birling Gap   Beachy Head

Bognor Regis

Selsey Bill

0   5   10   15   20 Miles

0   5   10   15   20   25   30 Kilometres

ENGLISH CHANNEL

M4   M3   M25   M26   M20   M23   A2   A12   A13   A127   A299   A259   A24   A27   A23   A22   A21

R Medway   R Mole   R Arun   R Adur   R Ouse   R Stour   Cuckmere River

INTRODUCTION

Aylesford
Kent

After being invited to Britain by the Romano-British ruler, Vortigern, to help defend Kent against the Picts, the Jutish mercenaries, Hengest and Horsa, rebelled and turned against the Britons. The two armies met at Aylesford in about AD 455 and in the battle which followed Horsa was killed. Hengest and his son, Asc, became co-rulers of the Jutish kingdom of Kent. Aylesford, with its medieval church and bridge, is situated at an important crossing-point on the Medway. A Carmelite friary was founded here in 1242 on land owned by Richard de Grey. After the Dissolution, the property passed into private ownership, but when it came up for sale in 1949 the Carmelites managed to regain their ancient home. Today the priory is an important centre of pilgrimage. At its entrance is a Latin inscription which translated means: 'The flower of Carmel, once cut down, now blooms again with greater splendour.' On the slopes of the North Downs, north-east of Aylesford, are two prehistoric burial chambers, Kit's Coty House and Little Kit's Coty House, both English Heritage.

The official inauguration of the Channel Tunnel on 6 May 1994 by Queen Elizabeth II and President Mitterrand of France focused world attention on south-east England as the 'Gateway to the Nation'. With the building and opening of the 31-mile tunnel – one of the great engineering projects of the century – the barrier between island Britain and mainland Europe was breached. For the first time in some 7,000 years it became possible to cross the Channel on dry land, a feat no less significant than Louis Blériot's historic flight across the Channel on 25 July 1909. Yet, despite media claims to the contrary, Britain still remains an island. It may be physically joined to the Continent, but what will always keep it apart are the time-honoured character and traditions of its people, the great diversity of its scenery, the rich heritage of its architecture and the wealth of its literary and artistic associations.

Like every other region in the island, south-east England has a quality all its own. The landscape, although rarely spectacular, has much that is typical of the idealized English scene: from close-grazed downland, dotted with sheep and serenaded by skylarks, to spacious village greens where cricket is played on lazy summer afternoons. But the feature most celebrated by writers and poets is the lushness and fertility of the countryside: 'Kent, sir' remarked Mr Jingle in Dickens' *Pickwick Papers*, 'everyone knows Kent – apples, cherries, hops and women.'

Although Kent is traditionally known as the Garden of England, the term could just as easily apply to Surrey and Sussex. In addition to orchards, vineyards and hop-fields, the region contains some of the island's greatest gardens: Sissinghurst, Great Dixter, Leonardslee, Claremont, Nymans, Sheffield Park, Wakehurst Place, Wisley. Many suffered badly from the great storm which wreaked havoc across the region in 1987, with hurricane-force winds toppling ancient trees, damaging historic buildings and changing the face of the landscape overnight. Thousands of acres of woodland were decimated, while much of the coast was battered by mountainous waves. It was not the first storm to ravage the region, nor was it the last. One of the worst on record struck in November 1703, and was recalled by the author and diarist John Evelyn:

> Methinks I still hear, sure I am that I feel, the dismal groans of our forests, when the late dreadful hurricane subverted so many thousands of good oaks, prostrating the trees, laying

them in ghastly postures, like whole regiments of soldiers fallen in battle by the sword of
    the Conqueror, and crushing all that grew beneath them.

Yet, however terrible the destruction, the scars have always healed and the landscape has gradually recovered.

The geology of the region is relatively simple and regular. Lying between the great chalk ridges of the North and South Downs, which stretch from Hampshire to the Channel coast, are the sands and clays of the Kent and Sussex Weald. Beyond the extremities of both Downs and Weald are the sands and clays of the Sussex Plain, the North Kent Plain and the London Basin. Thanet, in the north-east corner of Kent, is a separate outcrop of chalk. While north of Guildford are the sands of the Surrey heaths. The symmetrical pattern of the rock strata – the levels of Romney Marsh are mirrored at Pevensey, and the white cliffs of Dover and South Foreland are echoed at Beachy Head and the Seven Sisters – is due to the erosion of a great upfolded dome of chalk, known as the Wealden Anticline, which once joined the North Downs with the South Downs. Some rocks are more resistant to erosion than others, and in the Weald high ridges of sandstone alternate with valleys, or troughs, of softer clays. From the Central or High Weald, which rises to almost 800 feet at Crowborough Beacon, the rock strata spread out in sequence like ripples on a pond, the oldest in the middle and the youngest at the edges: Fairlight Clays, Hastings Beds, Weald Clay, Lower Greensand, Gault, Upper Greensand and Chalk. Before it was sliced through by the English Channel, the same land mass stretched into what is now northern France, so that white cliffs face each other across the Strait of Dover and under the seabed the Channel Tunnel follows a stratum of chalk.

In 1994, buried beneath rock layers that have accumulated over the millennia, Roger Pedersen unearthed the shin bone of what may be the oldest human remains in Europe. Since the early 1980s archaeologists have been excavating a quarry in Boxgrove, West Sussex, where evidence of ancient human activity half-a-million years ago has been found in the form of stone axes, flint tools and butchered animal bones. The discovery of the bone of so-called Boxgrove Man predates the fragments of a human skull found in 1935-6 near Swanscombe, Kent, by an incredible 250,000 years. But perhaps the region's most famous archaeological 'discovery' was made in 1912 by Charles Dawson, a lawyer, who bewildered scholars for over forty years with a skull unearthed at Piltdown, East Sussex, that was part-human part-ape. Believed to be the missing link between early humans and their ape ancestors, Piltdown Man was given the name *Eoanthropus dawsoni*, meaning 'Dawson's dawn man'. It was not until 1953, when scientific methods of testing had improved, that the skull was found to be a fraud: the jaw was that of an orang-utan and the skull that of a medieval human, both treated to appear fossilized.

Since prehistoric times, when Britain became an island, wave after wave of peoples from different parts of Europe have crossed the Channel and passed through the Gateway to the Nation: Mesolithic hunters, Neolithic settlers, Bronze Age farmers, Iron Age warriors, Roman legionaries, Jutish mercenaries, Christian missionaries, Saxon immigrants and Norman conquerors. Today, the opening of the Channel Tunnel has permitted a far more peaceful 'invasion', providing visitors from the Continent with fast and reliable access to the glories of the Garden of England: romantic ruins such as Bayham, Bodiam and Scotney; the cathedral cities of Canterbury and Chichester; Roman remains including the Pharos at Dover, the fort at Richborough and the palace at Fishbourne; magnificent castles like Hever, Leeds and Arundel; such princely residences as the Royal Pavilion at Brighton; the enigmatic chalk figure of the Long Man of Wilmington; historic houses such as Chartwell, Bateman's and Polesden Lacey; medieval cottages of which the Clergy House at Alfriston and the Priest House at West Hoathly are but two examples; and all – from the grandest to the humblest – set amidst some of the most fruitful countryside in England. Yet within the region the landscape varies considerably: from the wooded hills of Surrey to the bleak marshland of the Hoo Peninsular; from the undulating ridges of the North and South Downs to the coastal plains of North Kent and Chichester; and from the open heathland of Ashdown Forest to the perpendicular cliffs of Beachy Head.

Visitors from the Continent may no longer have to skirt the extensive and almost impenetrable forest of ancient Andreadsweald, which – until the trees were felled to build ships, smelt iron and make charcoal – once filled the Weald of Kent and Sussex. But they will find themselves amidst ground steeped in history: the landing of Hengest and Horsa near Sandwich in AD 449; the arrival of the Christian missionary St Augustine in 597; the momentous battle of Senlac Hill, near Hastings, in 1066; the murder of Thomas Becket at Canterbury in 1170; the signing of the Magna Carta at Runnymede in 1215; and, more recently, the Battle of Britain, fought over the skies of south-east England during the Second World War.

The opening of the Channel Tunnel in 1994 confirmed the Garden of England's status as the Gateway to the Nation. The region is now the main thoroughfare between London and the Continent. For those apt to linger there are treasures aplenty that should not be missed.

GUILDFORD AND SURREY

Gibbet Hill
Hindhead Common

Not far from the 895-foot-high summit of Gibbet Hill, two miles north of Haslemere, is a memorial stone, 'erected in detestation of a barbarous murder committed here on an unknown sailor on Sept. 24th. 1786'. The three villains responsible, James Marshall, Michael Casey and Edward Lonegon, were hung in chains from the gibbet which gave the hill its name. The young sailor's tombstone stands in the churchyard of St Michael and All Angels at Thursley, two miles north. On the western side of Gibbet Hill is a steep-sided sandstone depression, known as the Devil's Punch Bowl, which Cobbett called 'the most villainous spot that God ever made'. In *Nicholas Nickleby* (1839) Dickens wrote that 'the blood of the murdered man had run down, drop by drop, into the hollow which gives the place its name. "The Devil's Bowl", thought Nicholas, as he looked into the void, "never held fitter liquor than that."' Much of the area is now in the care of the National Trust. Nature Trails extend south to Grayswood Common, Stoatley Green and Black Down.

Every body that has been from Godalming to Guildford knows, that there is hardly another such a pretty four miles in all England. The road is good; the soil is good; the houses are neat; the people are neat; the hills, the woods, the meadows, all are beautiful. Nothing wild and bold to be sure: but exceedingly pretty; and it is almost impossible to ride along these four miles without feelings of pleasure.

William Cobbett wrote this in 1822, and much has changed over subsequent decades: the population has expanded; the motor car has replaced the horse and cart; suburbia has eroded the countryside; roads, railways and canals have sectioned the landscape, in some cases dividing whole communities; motorways have encouraged out-of-town shopping centres and business parks; and building development has altered the character of almost every town and village. Yet, despite its proximity to the great metropolis of London, the vast proportion of land in the South-East remains green and fertile. Little wonder that the region is celebrated as the Garden of England.

Strictly speaking, the Garden of England refers to the county of Kent, a district renowned for the richness and fertility of its soil, the abundance of its orchards, the glory of its gardens and the lushness of its meadows. Although Cobbett was born at Farnham in Surrey, he was not averse to calling the Wealden area between Maidstone and Tunbridge Wells 'the very finest, as to fertility and diminutive beauty, in this whole world'. Yet it was not a place where he wanted to live. 'I think nothing of it at all,' he wrote, 'compared with a country where high downs prevail, with here and there a large wood on the top or the side of a hill, and where you see, in the deep dells, here and there a farmhouse, and here and there a village, the buildings sheltered by a group of lofty trees.' Yet from his vantage point on the windswept heights of the gently, swelling downs, he could feast his eyes on the sumptuous countryside of the Weald, and thereby draw pleasure and inspiration from both.

It is precisely this sharply contrasting landscape of Downs and Weald – chalk adjoining sands and clays – that gives the Garden of England its unique and distinctive character. And the link that binds the two is, in the words of Surrey writer Eric Parker, 'a farmer's link, lime. For sand and clay alike, lime for centuries has been the fertiliser.' Chalk from the downs converted into lime and applied to the land to help sweeten the acid soils of the Weald. 'Perfick,' as Pop Larkin in *The Darling Buds of May* might say, 'Perfick.' But clay is not the easiest of soils to cultivate, and to be productive it requires generations of back-breaking labour and toil. 'Yet somehow crops were induced to grow,' wrote Ralph Lawrence, 'and a Wealden crop is a fine one, for clay rewards the exertion spent on its conquest.'

From the hills of Surrey to the hop-fields of Kent and the downlands of Sussex, the diversity of plant life is so dramatic and beautiful that it can hardly be rivalled anywhere else in England. The rivers that weave their gentle course through the ever-changing countryside contribute in part to the fertility of the region: the Adur, Arun, Ouse and Stour; the Medway, Cuckmere, Rother, Mole and Wey, plus many other smaller streams and tributaries, all eventually debouching into the sea. But, famed as the region is for its fruit-filled orchards, leaf-dappled woodland, open, turf-sprung sheep pastures and golden fields of ripening corn, it also contains a wealth and variety of gardens: the Royal Horticultural Society's trial grounds at Wisley, the 'outdoor rooms' at Sissinghurst. water gardens at Denmans, old fashioned roses at Nymans, spring-flowering shrubs at Leonardslee, ordered informality at Great Dixter, autumn vibrancy at Winkworth, lakes and waterfalls at Sheffield Park, herbaceous borders at West Dean, specimen conifers at Bedgebury National Pinetum, herbs at Iden Croft, daffodils and rhododendrons at Mount Ephraim and, far from exhausting the list, a unique turf amphitheatre at Claremont.

But, however wild and informal, gardens need gardeners. As Rudyard Kipling wrote:

> Our England is a garden, and such gardens are not made
> By singing: – 'Oh, how beautiful!' and sitting in the shade.

Kipling designed and planted much of Bateman's, his home from 1902 until his death in 1936. Others who have contributed to the region's botanical treasures include: landscape designers and gardeners like Lancelot 'Capability' Brown (1716-83), Charles Bridgeman (d. 1738), William Kent (1685-1748) and Humphry Repton (1752-1818); exotic plant-collectors such as Joseph Banks (1743-1820), one of the founders of the Royal Horticultural Society; garden designers like Gertrude Jekyll (1843-1932) and William Robinson (1838-1935), both of whom favoured 'natural' gardens; and those not primarily associated with gardens like John Evelyn (1620-1706), John Vanbrugh (1664-1726), Edwin Lutyens (1869-1944) and Vita Sackville-West (1892-1962).

With such dedicated and creative talent, it is not surprising that these plant-filled oases within the Garden of England are revered by millions.

Semaphore Tower
Chatley Heath

During the late eighteenth and early nineteenth centuries – when England was under threat of a French invasion – a chain of hill-top telegraph stations was established as a visual communications link between the naval base at Portsmouth and the Admiralty in London. The 60-foot high, brick semaphore tower on top of Chatley Heath was erected in 1822 to replace a shutter telegraph built of wood. Messages were relayed to the next station down the line by means of two pivoting arms, attached, one above the other, to a 30-foot mast. Cobbett chanced upon one of these 'queer-looking buildings' in October 1825.

> This building is, it seems, called a *Semaphore*, or *Semiphare*, or something of that sort. What this word may have been hatched out of I cannot say; but it means *a job*, I am sure. To call it an *alarm-post* would not have been so convenient.... *Alarm-post* would be a nasty name; and it would puzzle people exceedingly, when they saw one.

The 'alarm-post' at Chatley Heath was closed down in 1847. Reduced to a burnt-out shell in 1984, it was fully restored in 1989.

Amphitheatre
Claremont Landscape Garden

One of the earliest landscape gardens in England, Claremont was begun by Sir John Vanbrugh, who purchased the site in 1708. Three years later the property was sold to Thomas Pelham-Holles, later Earl of Clare and Duke of Newcastle. Further landscaping of the enlarged estate was carried out by Charles Bridgeman, who in 1726 designed the turf amphitheatre, consisting of a semi-circle of five steep terraces, centred around an oval 'stage', with three further terraces descending in a fan beneath. The white benches are copies of eighteenth-century garden furniture. The original pond was made into a lake in the 1730s by William Kent, who further enhanced and extended the site by planting trees and building a simple ha-ha. Additional improvements were carried out by 'Capability' Brown, who was also commissioned by Lord Clive to build a new house on the site of Vanbrugh's 'very small box' of 1708. The house was completed in 1774, with the assistance of Henry Holland and John Soane and is now used as a school. The garden has been restored by the National Trust.

Wisley Garden

In 1904, on the centenary of its foundation, the Royal Horticultural Society (RHS) moved from its site at Chiswick to Wisley, some two miles south of Byfleet. The original 60-acre estate was owned by George Ferguson Wilson, who cultivated only a small part of it as a garden, 'a place where plants from all over the world grow wild'. After his death in 1902, the estate was purchased by Sir Thomas Hanbury and given to the RHS. Today the world-famous garden covers some 250 acres and features all aspects of gardening, including trial grounds where the merits of different varieties of flowers, woody plants and vegetables can be determined. Types of garden range from rock to rose and from wild to woodland. There is even a specialist garden for disabled people. With glasshouses and landscaped areas containing over 40,000 plants, Wisley Garden has an international reputation for horticultural excellence. The half-timbered house, now converted into offices and laboratories, was built in 1914 by Imrie and Angell. Facilities for visitors include a restaurant, café, shop and plant centre.

Hatchlands

Just east of the village of East Clandon, the striking red-brick Palladian house at Hatchlands Park was built in 1757 by Stiff Leadbetter for Admiral Edward Boscawen, who helped British troops capture the French stronghold of Louisbourg, Cape Breton Island, Nova Scotia, on 26 July 1758 and was known to his men as 'Old Dreadnought'. It was Boscawen and his wife who gave Robert Adam his first commission: to decorate part of the interior, notably the Library and Drawing Room. Later alterations included the flat pilastered doorway on the west front by Joseph Bonomi, dating from the late eighteenth century, and the single-storey Music Room of about 1903 by Sir Reginald Blomfield. The exterior is remarkable in that the west front has three storeys, while the south front has two. The house, garden and park were given to the National Trust in 1945. Hatchlands now contains the Alec Cobbe collection of paintings, furniture and keyboard instruments. Humphry Repton (1752-1818) and Gertrude Jekyll (1843-1932) were involved in the design of the gardens.

Clandon Park

Standing on the site of an earlier house, three miles east of Guildford, Clandon was built in the Palladian style for Thomas, second Baron Onslow, by the Venetian architect, Giacomo Leoni, in the early 1730s. Consisting of a solid red-brick rectangle with stone dressings, the house stands in grounds landscaped by 'Capability' Brown in about 1770. The two-storeyed marble entrance hall, with its rich decoration and fine plasterwork ceiling, was considered by Ian Nairn to be 'one of the grandest early Palladian rooms in England'. Now in the care of the National Trust, the house contains portraits of the Onslow family, three of whom served as Speakers of the House of Commons; a magnificent collection of furniture, porcelain and needlework bequeathed by Hannah Gubbay in 1969; and the Ivo Forde collection of Meissen Italian comedy figures. In the basement is the Queen's Royal Surrey Regimental Museum. The brightly painted Maori House in the grounds was brought from New Zealand by William, fourth Earl Onslow, who was governor of the islands from 1888 to 1892.

Guildford Castle

Originating as a river-crossing settlement, the old market town of Guildford was first recorded in a ninth-century document as Gyldeforda, meaning the 'golden ford'. Towards the end of the eleventh century the Normans erected a motte-and-bailey castle on a prominent site dominating the town. The square keep, standing high on the east bank of the River Wey, dates from the middle of the twelfth century. During the following century the castle became more important as a royal palace than a fortress. Today the inner bailey is a public park with gardens, bowling green and bandstand. Abutting Castle Arch, thought to have been built in 1256, is a local history museum with exhibits relating to Charles Lutwidge Dodgson (Lewis Carroll), who died in 1898 at The Chestnuts, Castle Hill – the home of his six unmarried sisters. He was buried, across the Wey, in the old Mount cemetery. Sir Thomas Malory, the fifteenth-century author of *Le Morte d'Arthur*, thought that the town was the Astolat of Arthurian legends, the dwelling place of Elaine the White (Tennyson's Lady of Shalott), who died of love for Lancelot.

River Wey
Guildford

Work on making the River Wey navigable from Weybridge, on the Thames, to Guildford was completed in 1653, but the extension to Godalming, four-and-a-half miles upstream, remained closed to river traffic until about a century later. The twenty-mile-long waterway ceased to be used commercially in about 1918 and is now in the care of the National Trust. Not far from the Jolly Farmer riverside inn (shown in the photograph) are the Guildford Boathouse, offering boats for hire, pleasure trips and a cruising restaurant, and the Yvonne Arnaud Theatre, opened in 1965. High on Stag Hill, overlooking the river, town and castle ruins, is Guildford Cathedral, started in 1936, consecrated in 1961 and completed in 1966. Designed by Sir Edward Maufe, it is one of very few Anglican cathedrals to be built in Britain since the Reformation. The medieval Pilgrim's Way, stretching from Winchester to Canterbury, crosses the river just south of the town, where it passes, on St Catherine's Hill, the ruins of an early fourteenth-century chapel.

Polesden Lacey

Richard Brinsley Sheridan, the politician and playwright, purchased Polesden Lacey in 1797, describing it as 'the nicest place, within a prudent distance of town, in England'. The early seventeenth-century house was replaced in the 1820s by a Regency villa built by Joseph Bonsor to the designs of Thomas Cubitt. The building was much enlarged after 1902 by Ambrose Poynter. Four years later, the property was purchased by Ronald Greville and his wife Margaret, daughter of the wealthy brewer, William McEwan. A celebrated society hostess, Mrs Greville's parties at the house were attended by the rich and famous, including King Edward VII. In 1923, for part of their honeymoon, she lent the house to the Duke and Duchess of York (future King George VI and Queen Elizabeth). On her death in 1942, Mrs Greville left the Polesden estate to the National Trust, including her outstanding collection of silver and porcelain. Nairn said of Poynter's interior: 'Its character is now entirely Edwardian, and, be it said, some of the most attractive Edwardian in the country.'

St James' Well
Abinger Common

Opposite Goddards, a house built by Edwin Lutyens in 1898-9, is St James' Well, opened for the use of Abinger parishioners in 1893. The Norman church of St James at Abinger Common was largely destroyed by a flying bomb in 1944 and restored by Frederick Etchells. Further restoration was carried out after the tower was damaged by lightning in 1964. Near the Manor House is a Stone Age (Mesolithic) pit-dwelling, dating from about 5000 BC. On the Abinger Hammer-to-Dorking road is Crossways Farm, featured in George Meredith's novel *Diana of the Crossways* (1885). To the north on Abinger Roughs is a large granite memorial to Samuel Wilberforce, Bishop of Winchester from 1869 to 1873. It marks the spot where he was thrown from his horse and killed. At St James' Church in nearby Shere are the remains of the cell in which the anchoress, Christine Carpenter, was voluntarily enclosed in 1329, 'that therein she may be able to serve Almighty God the more worthily'. Preserved inside the church is a tiny bronze madonna and child, dug up by a dog on Juniper Hill, Combe Bottom, in about 1880.

Village Green
Brockham

At the confluence of the River Mole and the Tanner's Brook, the village of Brockham is set around a spacious green on which the legendary W.G. Grace is said to have played cricket. At the southern end of the green, near Vicarage Cottage, is the parish church, built in 1846 by Benjamin Ferry in thirteenth-century cruciform style. Each November the green is the setting for what is claimed to be the biggest Guy Fawkes bonfire in Surrey. Near the entrance to Brockham Court Farm is a brick-built pound, with a plaque saying: 'Brockham's own Act of Parliament (1812) allowed only poultry to depasture the green. Cattle or horses were impounded until a fine had been paid to the Lord of the Manor.' The Dukes Head inn, overlooking the green, serves as a reminder that the Dukes of Norfolk used to stop overnight at Brockham on their journey from London to Arundel. At Brockham Quarries, in the scarp of the North Downs, are the remains of nineteenth-century lime kilns, in use until the 1930s. From the summit of Box Hill overlooking Brockham are extensive views over Surrey and Sussex.

Abinger Hammer

On the Guildford-to-Dorking road, north-west of Abinger Common, this village takes the second part of its name not from the hammer-clock (shown in the photograph) but from the 'hammer ponds' formed during Elizabethan times by damming the Tillingbourne river. Abinger Hammer was a notable area of the Wealden iron industry, and the ponds were used to store water for driving the water-wheels which powered the trip hammers in the forges. During the late nineteenth century the ponds were found to be ideal for growing watercress. The clock, overhanging the winding main road, stands on the site of a forge, and, appropriately, the time is marked by the figure of a blacksmith striking the bell with his hammer. It bears the mottos: 'For you at home I part the day, twixt sleep & meals & work & play' and 'By me you know how fast to go'. E.M. Forster (1879-1970), whose *Abinger Harvest*, a collection of essays, was published in 1936, lived at the house in the village called West Hackhurst. On his death he left Piney Copse, some four acres of woodland, to the National Trust.

St John's Church
Wotton

The church of St John the Evangelist at Wotton, three miles west of Dorking, stands on high ground facing the North Downs. John Evelyn, born at Wotton House in 1620, wrote in his *Diary* that the place was 'so sweetly environed with those delicious streams and venerable woods, as in the judgement of Strangers as well as Englishmen it may be compared to one of the most pleasant seats in the nation'. Inside the church, with its early Norman tower topped by a two-stage pyramid roof, are various memorials to the Evelyn family, including one to George Evelyn, who died in 1603 and is represented with two wives and twenty-four children. The remains of the diarist, who died in 1706, are above ground in a simple coffin-shaped monument in the Evelyn Chapel. His wife, Mary, who succeeded him by three years, lies nearby. On the inner arch of the south doorway are eight little carved heads, said to represent a variety of thirteenth-century characters, great and small, including the main protagonists in a quarrel that King John had with the Pope over the election of Stephen Langton as Archbishop of Canterbury in 1206-13.

Holmbury Hill
near Holmbury St Mary

Enclosing the 857-foot-high summit of Holmbury Hill are the bracken- and bramble-covered ramparts of a roughly square Iron Age hill-fort, about eight acres in extent. Excavation has established that the camp was built shortly before the Roman Conquest. The photograph was taken from the summit looking west across the tree-clad greensand ridge towards Pitch Hill. Cobbett rode along the bottom of the ridge in August 1823 and, because of the deep clay, it took him a good hour-and-a-half to travel three miles: 'Now, mind, this is the real *weald* where the clay is *bottomless*; where there is no stone of any sort underneath.' Sited on the slopes of a steep wooded valley to the north-east, Holmbury St Mary developed during Victorian times out of a small hamlet called Felday. St Mary's, built in 1879, was one of the last churches to be designed by George Edmund Street, the architect responsible for the Law Courts in London, and was built at his own expense in memory of his second wife. He lived on the side of Holmbury Hill in the tile-hung and half-timbered house, Holmdale.

Post Mill
Outwood

Built in 1665, the post mill at Outwood, five miles south-east of Reigate, is the oldest working windmill in England. Standing 400 feet above sea-level, the mill once had a rival: a smock mill said to have been built in 1790 by Ezekiel in an attempt to force his brother, Isaac, out of business. The attempt failed, partly because of ill-fortune and partly because of Ezekiel's all too frequent visits to the local tavern. Although it fell into disrepair, the smock mill survived until 1960, when it was destroyed by a storm. Travelling through Reigate from Guildford in 1722-3, Defoe praised the countryside as being 'agreeably pleasant, wholesome and fruitful'. To the south, however, he noted that all

is exceedingly grown with tim-ber, has abundance of waste and wild grounds, and forests and woods, with many large iron-works, at which they cast great quantities of iron cauldrons, chimney-backs, furnaces, retorts, boiling pots, and all the neces-sary things of iron; besides iron cannon, bomb-shells, stink-pots, hand-grenadoes [sic], and can-non ball, &c.

Church of St Peter and St Paul
Ewhurst

The sandstone church of St Peter and St Paul, standing on a small knoll above the straggling village of Ewhurst, dates from Norman times but was much rebuilt in the early thirteenth, fifteenth and sixteenth centuries. The tower collapsed in 1837, damaging the chancel and north transept, and was rebuilt in the Norman style with a broached spire by Robert Ebbels. At the same time parts of the exterior were given a flint dressing, traditionally placed to cut the devil if he came too close. Restoration in 1931 involved the spire being re-shingled, and before application, many of the individual shingles were signed by the parishioners. The seventeenth-century altar rails, originally at nearby Baynard's Park, are claimed to be the finest in Surrey. On the north side of the churchyard is a gravestone damaged by the falling tower. Overlooking the village to the north is the 843-foot-high Pitch Hill. The brick windmill, close by, ceased work in 1885 and was converted into a house in 1901. In its heyday it was apparently used as a depot by smugglers.

Leith Hill Tower

Crowning the highest point in south-east England, Leith Hill Tower was erected in 1765 by Richard Hull, a Bristol merchant, whose body was later buried beneath its floor. In 1796 the tower was heightened, while the octagonal turret with its spiral staircase was added in 1864. Rising to 1,092 feet above sea-level, the views from the top are extensive, with glimpses of London to the north and the English Channel to the south. Leith Hill Place dates from the early seventeenth century and was owned by Hull. It subsequently belonged to the Wedgwood and Vaughan Williams families, until Ralph Vaughan Williams gave it to the National Trust in 1945. Ockley, two miles south of the hill, is claimed by some to be the unidentified Aclea, mentioned in the *Anglo-Saxon Chronicle*, where in 851 the Saxon army under Ethelwulf, King of Wessex, defeated the Danes and 'made the greatest slaughter of a heathen host that we have ever heard tell of'. Anstiebury Iron Age hill-fort, north-east of Leith Hill, is one of the largest in Surrey.

Winkworth Arboretum

Some three miles south-east of Godalming, the 99-acre hillside site of Winkworth Arboretum – with its two lakes, 'Alpine Meadow' and sweeping views over the North Downs – was largely created by Dr Wilfrid Fox, who acquired much of the land in 1937 and planted it with rare trees and shrubs. Carpeted with bluebells and shimmering with blossom in spring, during the autumn the arboretum is ablaze with foliage that varies from rich scarlet to brilliant yellow, with soft greens, blues and browns providing a striking contrast. It is now in the care of the National Trust, and its varied habitats provide a haven for birds such as woodpeckers, nuthatches, kingfishers and herons. On the 593-foot-high summit of Hydon's Ball, two miles south-west, is a large granite seat commemorating the fact that much of the surrounding heath and woodland was acquired by the National Trust in 1915 as a memorial to Octavia Hill (1838-1912), one of its three co-founders. On Hascombe Hill, to the east, are the earthwork remains of an Iron Age promontory fort, thought to date from the late first century BC.

Waverley Abbey

Beside the River Wey, two miles south-east of Farnham, the first Cistercian house in England, Waverley Abbey, was founded in 1128 by William Giffard, Bishop of Winchester. It was suppressed in 1536 and subsequently plundered for its building materials. Among the fragments which survive today are the ruins of the vaulted thirteenth-century *cellarium*, or great storehouse (shown in the photograph). The site is now in the care of English Heritage. It is from here that Sir Walter Scott is said to have taken the title of his first novel *Waverley* published in 1814. William Cobbett was born at the Jolly Farmer (now William Cobbett), Farnham, in 1763. Sixty-three years later he revisited Waverley and 'found the ruins not very greatly diminished'. Finding the cave of Mother Ludlam, the white witch of Waverley, he wrote: 'Alas! It is not the enchanting place that I knew it, nor which Grose describes in his Antiquities!' In 1696-7 Jonathan Swift, while staying at nearby Moor Park, the home of Sir William Temple, wrote *A Tale of a Tub* and *The Battle of the Books*.

Frensham Little Pond
Frensham Common

The National Trust owns about 1000 acres of Frensham Common, including the two artificial lakes – Frensham Great Pond and Frensham Little Pond – originally created in the early thirteenth century to provide fish for the estate of the Bishop of Winchester. During the Second World War they were drained to stop enemy bombers using them as navigation markers. Less than a mile south-east, near Churt, are three conical hills known as the Devil's Jumps of which Cobbett wrote:

> For my part, I cannot account for the placing of these hills. That they should have been formed by mere chance is hardly to be believed. How could waters rolling about have formed such hills? How could such hills have bubbled up from beneath? But, in short, it is all wonderful alike.

It is now known that the hills owe their appearance to a capping of resistant ironstone. St Mary's Church at Frensham contains a beaten copper cauldron, estimated to hold 100 gallons, which tradition claims either belonged to the Waverley witch, Mother Ludlam, or the monks of Waverley Abbey.

Horsham and the Sussex Weald

The Causeway
Horsham

On the edge of St Leonard's Forest and in the heart of the western Weald, the medieval borough and market town of Horsham grew up around a wedge-shaped green, eventually overrun by permanent buildings. The only open space that now survives is the Carfax, or crossroads, in the north and the Causeway, a long tapering tree-lined street, in the south. The latter, which contains some of the finest timber-framed town houses in Sussex, leads to the church of St Mary the Virgin, where a simple tablet commemorates the son of a former MP for Horsham, Percy Bysshe Shelley, who was born in 1792 at Field Place, a mile or so west of the town. Although the tablet was placed in the church as part of the Shelley centenary celebrations in 1892, there was little enthusiasm among the parishioners for a memorial to the atheist poet. Causeway House, a sixteenth-century town house with parts dating from 1460, serves as the town museum.

In the not so distant past the richly wooded Wealden countryside around Horsham was renowned as the haunt of dragons. 'True and Wonderful', proclaimed the title of a pamphlet published in 1614, adding by way of explanation:

> A Discourse relating to a strange monstrous Serpent or Dragon, lately discovered and yet living, to the great annoyance and divers slaughters both of Men and Cattle, by his strong and violent Poison, in Sussex, two miles from Horsham, in a Wood called St. Leonard's Forest, and thirty miles from London.

This black-scaled, red-bellied and possibly large-footed creature was reported to be

> some nine feet, or rather more, in length, and shaped almost in the form of an axletree of a cart, a quantity of thickness in the midst, and somewhat smaller at both ends. He is of countenance very proud, and at the sight or hearing of men or cattle will raise his neck upright, and seem to listen and look about with great arrogancy.

The report goes on to say that a man and a woman were slain by its venom at a distance of about 66 feet, and, when discovered, their bodies were found to be 'poisoned and much swelled, but not preyed upon'. Among the witnesses who vouched for the truth of the account was 'the carrier of Horsham, who lyeth at the White Horse in Southwark'!

Tales of strange beasts are particularly bountiful in the region. In addition to accounts of monstrous snakes, serpents and dragon-like creatures, one of which was said to have been shot at Haywards Heath in 1794, there have been persistent reports of large cats roaming the countryside. William Cobbett, when a small boy, was scolded, then beaten, for insisting that he had seen a cat 'as big as a middle-sized spaniel' at Waverley. Sightings of the so-called 'Surrey Puma' reached a peak in the 1960s, with the police issuing a warning for the public to keep away from heathland near Peaslake. Many of the stories about monsters, ghosts and fairies were put to good use by smugglers, who were far from averse to creating a few of their own. On Romney Marsh, for instance, there is the gruesome tale of a smuggler, believed to have turned informant, who was murdered as a warning to those who might follow his example. On certain nights, perhaps when contraband was on the move, his ghost was said to wander restlessly through the countryside, searching in vain for the scattered parts of his dismembered body.

Unlike 'fair-traders' elsewhere in Britain, the smugglers in south-east England had a particularly savage reputation. At its height in the late eighteenth and nineteenth centuries, smuggling in the region was carried out by large and highly organized gangs, in the face of which the forces of law and order were powerless to act. The level of violence and lawlessness reached such proportions that entire areas came under the absolute control of the gangs and their adherents. Many of these gangs, however, were eventually brought to justice for murder rather than for smuggling. These included the North Kent Gang led by James West, who ended up dancing 'the hempen jig' on the gallows at Penenden Heath near Maidstone, and the notorious Hawkhurst Gang, whose activities under the leadership of the infamous Thomas Kingsmill extended from 'fair-trading' to terrorizing virtually the whole of Kent and Sussex.

Fear, particularly of the unknown, has not only been inspired by places on land. In the English Channel, four miles off the coast at Deal, lie the treacherous Goodwin Sands, where 50,000 mariners are believed to have perished in shipwrecks. Not surprisingly, the waters around the sands – reputedly the site of the drowned island of Lomea – are said to be haunted. Perhaps the most famous of the Goodwin ghost ships is the *Lady Lovibond*, a three-masted schooner which ran aground in February 1748 to vanish without trace, presumably sucked down into the sands of the notorious 'Shippe Swallower'. It was said afterwards that the ship's mate, in a fit of jealous rage, had deliberately wrecked the vessel because the girl he loved had married the captain. From time to time, like several other phantom ships, the *Lady* allegedly returns from the past to re-enact the disaster.

Another stretch of water, also reputed to be haunted, is the Silent Pool, near Shere in Surrey. Legend says that a mounted stranger brought about the death of a woodcutter's two children – both of whom were unable to swim – by causing them to drown in the deepest part of the pool. After their father had dragged their lifeless bodies from the water, he discovered a feather from the stranger's hat caught in a tree, thereby deducing that his offspring had been murdered. Subsequent enquiries led to the stranger being identified as none other than King John. It is said that the public outcry over the deaths of the two children led to the barons uniting against the king, and ultimately forcing him to sign the Magna Carta at Runnymede in 1215. On a moonlit night, if the conditions are right, the naked girl may be seen entering the water and, before vanishing into the depths, heard to utter a wild, unearthly cry.

Ghosts, giants, witches, fairies, saints, angels and heroes – all make their appearance in the region's rich treasury of folklore and legends. A great many stories also feature the devil, who – apart from giving his name to such places as the Devil's Dyke, the Devil's

Punchbowl and the Devil's Jumps – is found near Midhurst throwing rocks at the god Thor, at Mayfield battling against St Dunstan and at Newington attempting to steal the church bells. Some tales of the supernatural and the unexplained are based on historical events. At Horsham in 1735, for example, John Weekes, the 'Dumb Man' of Fittleworth, was executed for murder. Instead of being hanged, however, he was slowly crushed to death by having large weights placed on his body. The executioner, who delivered the final act by standing on the pile himself, apparently dropped the corpse on its way to burial in the cemetery. A few days later, so the story goes, the executioner dropped down dead at exactly the same spot. A more recent example is the account of a motorist who gave a lift to a girl hitchhiking on the London-to-Worthing road. During the journey, she told him the address of her parents. Feeling in need of refreshment, the driver stopped at a café in Horsham. His passenger, however, refused to get out, so he left her in the vehicle. On his return he found that the girl had disappeared. Plagued by feelings that something terrible might have happened to her, he contacted her parents only to be told that their daughter had died three years earlier, run over while hitching a lift outside the very same café.

Like Horsham, many of the ancient towns and villages in south-east England are steeped in folklore, myth and legend. The customs, beliefs and traditions of the people are as much a product of historical events as they are of the geographical environment. As people continue to shape and influence the landscape, so the landscape continues to shape and influence them. Age-old stories of the locality, however fanciful or fantastic, continue to fascinate. In these so-called enlightened times most, if not all, may be dismissed as superstitious nonsense. Yet, stubbornly, they endure partly because of their richness and variety but mainly because they are a living force – an integral part of the spirit and character of the region's people.

'Please', beseeched Arthur Beckett in 1911, 'do not call them fairy stories. Unless you believe them as I do you cannot properly understand the Wonderful Weald. The simple spirit of old-time Sussex is the only spirit in which a man or woman can understand the county.' Or, for that matter, the South-East.

The Weald
from Black Down

At 919 feet above sea-level, the summit of Black Down is the highest point in Sussex, higher than any part of the South Downs. Situated a mile or so south of Haslemere, at the western end of the Weald, the sandstone (or, more accurately, Lower Greensand) ridge supports trees and plants favouring a dry acid soil: heather, bilberry, gorse, silver birch and Scots pine. Oak, whitebeam and rowan predominate on the steeper eastern slopes. The views from the summit are extensive, with villages and farmsteads seeming to occupy clearings in what was once a single vast forest. In 1868 Alfred, Lord Tennyson began building his country retreat on a heather-covered ledge near the top of the ridge, naming the house 'Aldworth' after his wife's home village in Berkshire. In his *Prologue to General Hamley* he wrote of her pleasure in the vista across the Weald:

> You came, and look'd and loved
>   the view
> Long-known and loved by me,
> Green Sussex fading into blue
> With one gray glimpse of sea.

He died in the house in 1892 and was buried in Westminster Abbey.

Cowdray House
Cowdray Park

On the north bank of the River Rother, opposite Midhurst, stand the battlemented ruins of Cowdray House, first built by Sir David Owen in the early sixteenth century. In 1529 the property was purchased by Sir William FitzWilliam (later Earl of Southampton), who made further improvements, such as the addition of the gatehouse and hexagonal tower. After FitzWilliam's death in 1542 the house passed to his half-brother, Sir Anthony Browne, who, through his friendship with Henry VIII, acquired several religious houses at the Dissolution, including Easebourne Priory, near Cowdray, Bayham Abbey near Tunbridge Wells, and Battle Abbey near Hastings. Legend holds, possibly in retrospect, that the last abbot of Battle Abbey laid a curse on the new owner, prophesying that his line would perish by fire and water. Fulfilment came in 1793, with the death by drowning in Germany of the eighth and last Lord Montague, and the destruction of the house by fire. Not far from the Tudor ruins is the world-famous Cowdray Park polo ground.

West Street
Midhurst

The old market town of
Midhurst, on the southern banks
of the River Rother, derives its
name from its situation 'amid
wooded hills': more specifically,
between the forested chalk
downs to the south and the tree-
covered sandstone hills to the
north. Just east of the church
of St Mary Magdalene and
St Denys, on St Ann's Hill,
the Normans built a castle, but
only traces of it remain. On the
corner of West Street and South
Street is the Spread Eagle Hotel,
a coaching inn dating from the
early fifteenth century with a
seven-bay front of about 1700.
The sixteenth-century Market
Hall housed the town's first
Grammar School, founded in
1672. Later pupils included
the novelist H.G. Wells
(1866-1946); the politician
and economist Richard Cobden
(1804-65), co-founder of the
Anti-Corn Law League; and
the geologist Charles Lyell
(1797-1875). According to local
legend a traveller who had been
overtaken by nightfall was led
to Midhurst and safety by the
sound of the church bell. The
event is commemorated at eight
each night by the ringing of the
curfew bell, now electronically
operated.

Shipley Mill

Standing just west of the
Wealden village of Shipley is
the largest smock mill in Sussex,
built in 1879 and variously
known as King's Mill, Vincent's
Mill, Belloc's Mill or, more
quaintly, Mrs Shipley. It was
fully restored to working order
in 1958 in memory of Hilaire
Belloc who lived in the
neighbouring house called King's
Land from 1906 – when he
purchased the mill – up to his
death in 1953. Belloc was buried
with his wife and son in the
cemetery of the Catholic church
of Our Lady of Consolation
at West Grinstead, a few miles
away. The churchyard at Shipley
itself contains the grave of the
composer, John Ireland (1879-
1962), who lived six miles
south at Washington and whose
works include *The Forgotten
Rite* (1913), *Legend* (1933) and
Sarnia (1941). Two miles north-
west of Shipley, at Coolham,
is a half-timbered farmhouse,
curiously called 'The Blue
Idol', part of which is a Quaker
meeting-house, associated with
William Penn, who lived four
miles south at Warminghurst
and in 1682 established a
colony for persecuted Quakers
in Pennsylvania, America.

Leonardslee Gardens

Set in a deep sheltered valley, five miles south-east of Horsham, the spectacular woodland gardens at Leonardslee were first planted in the early part of the nineteenth century. In 1852 the estate was purchased by William Egerton Hubbard, who erected the present mansion on the site of an earlier house. Although further planting took place, it was not until 1889, when Sir Edmund Loder acquired the estate, that Leonardslee began to take on the character for which it is justly celebrated today – an ever-changing landscape ranging from the vibrant colours of bluebells, azaleas and rhododendrons in spring to the shimmering golds and russets of maples, hickories and tupelos in autumn. The rock garden (shown in the picture) was laid out in about 1900. After Sir Edmund's death the Loder family carried on developing the 240-acre grounds, which include six lakes (a chain of old hammer ponds), waterfalls, woodland walks and parkland. Living semi-wild in parts of Leonardslee are wallabies, introduced in 1889, and three species of deer – sika, axis and fallow.

Winter Garden
Wakehurst Place

The gardens at Wakehurst Place, four miles north of Haywards Heath, were largely created by Gerald Loder (later Lord Wakehurst), who purchased the estate in 1903 and was the younger brother of Sir Edmund Loder of Leonardslee. Loder built up a magnificent collection of exotic plants, and after his death in 1936 the next owner, Sir Henry Price, continued the gardens' development. Although the property was bequeathed to the National Trust in 1964, the Elizabethan mansion and gardens have been administered and maintained by the Royal Botanical Gardens at Kew since 1965. Laid out in a large horseshoe, Wakehurst is particularly noted for its rare trees and flowering shrubs. Features include the Winter Garden, the Himalayan Glade, the Trans-Asian Heath Garden, the Memorial Garden, Horsebridge and Bethlehem Woods, the Water Garden, and Westwood Valley or the Ravine. Like many other gardens in the Sussex Weald, Wakehurst suffered severe damage from the storm of 1987. The Loder Valley Reserve, adjoining, supports a rich variety of habitats for plants and wildlife.

Standen House

Two miles south of East Grinstead, with superb views over Weirwood Reservoir to Ashdown Forest, Standen House was built in 1892-4 as a spacious country retreat for James Beale, a London solicitor. Considered to be one of the finest and best-preserved examples of the work of the architect Philip Webb – a long-standing friend and professional associate of William Morris – the house was designed around a medieval farmhouse and made inventive use of a variety of traditional and local building materials: brick, pebble-dash, timber, tile and stone. The white tower, containing the water tanks, contrasts strikingly with stone walls, tile-hung upper storeys, weather-boarded gables and tall brick chimney-stacks. Inside, Standen contains Morris-designed textiles and wallpapers, mostly original, and pottery by William de Morgan. The richly furnished, yet light and airy rooms were lit from the beginning by electricity and preserve many of the original fittings. The property and over 121 acres of surrounding land was bequeathed to the National Trust by Helen Beale in 1973.

Sheffield Park Garden

Watered by a tributary of the River Ouse, the 100-acre garden at Sheffield Park was laid out towards the end of the eighteenth century by 'Capability' Brown for John Baker Holroyd, later first Earl of Sheffield. In 1909, on the death of the third Earl, it was acquired by Arthur Gilstrap Soames, who transformed Brown's design, which included a chain of four lakes, into one of the most celebrated woodland gardens in Britain. The neo-Gothic mansion overlooking the park was designed by James Wyatt in 1775. Although the estate was purchased by the National Trust in 1954, the house and surrounding land remain in private ownership. At Sheffield Park Station, to the west, is the headquarters of the Bluebell Railway, which operates a vintage steam train service to and from Kingscote, via Horsted Keynes. Open all year, it boasts the largest collection of locomotives and carriages in the south of England, the earliest dating from 1865. The hamlet of Piltdown, to the south-east, is famous for the discovery of 'Piltdown Man', which turned out to be a colossal hoax.

Priest House
West Hoathly

Set high on a ridge, West Hoathly is noted for its timber-framed Priest House, dating from the early fifteenth century. Built by the Cluniac monks of Lewes Priory, it is now a folk museum owned by the Sussex Archaeological Society. The building has a Horsham slab roof and is surrounded by a traditional English cottage garden. St Margaret's Church, nearby, contains cast-iron tomb-slabs dating from the early seventeenth century when the village was a centre of the iron industry. Iron nails in the door spell out 'MARCH 31 1626'. The churchyard is terraced and offers views across the Weald to the South Downs. To the north of the village, Gravetye Manor (now a hotel) was built around 1600 by the Wealden ironmaster, Richard Infeld. From 1884 until his death in 1935, it was the home of the garden reformer, William Robinson. On the road between Turners Hill and Lindfield, near West Hoathly, Cobbett mentioned a large rock, balanced upon a smaller one, known as 'Big-upon-Little'. 'How, then, came this big upon little?' he asked, to no avail.

Ashdown Forest

In 1924, four years after the birth of his son, Christopher Robin, A.A. Milne published a book of children's verses entitled *When We Were Very Young.* The following year he purchased Cotchford, a red-brick farm-house, near Hartfield, on the edge of Ashdown Forest. Before Christopher left for boarding school in 1929, Milne wrote three more books in the series: *Winnie-the-Pooh* (1926), *Now We Are Six* (1927) and *The House at Pooh Corner* (1928). The landscape inhabited by Winnie-the-Pooh and his friends – Piglet, Eeyore, Kanga, Roo, Tigger and Co.- was inspired by Ashdown Forest. The existing Five Hundred Acre Wood, for example, became One Hundred Acre Wood, with Owl's House on its northern edge. Pooh Sticks Bridge, illustrated by E.H. Shepard, spans a small tributary of the River Medway, between Upper Hartfield and Posingford Wood. On Gills Lap, overlooking the open heathland with its clumps of Scots pines, is a memorial to Milne and Shepard, 'who collaborated in the creation of "Winnie-the-Pooh" and so captured the magic of Ashdown Forest and gave it to the world'.

Nymans Garden

Set on elevated ground amidst the scattered woodland of the Weald, some five miles south of Crawley, the internationally celebrated garden at Nymans contains the gutted shell of a pseudo-medieval manor built by Sir Walter Tapper in the 1920s for Lieutenant-Colonel Leonard Messel. Much of the house was destroyed by fire in 1947 and never rebuilt. The garden, with its magnificent collection of rare plants, shrubs and trees, was begun by Ludwig Messel in the 1890s. His son, Leonard, continued its development, sponsoring plant-collecting expeditions to various parts of the world. Leonard's wife, Maud, created the rose garden, which was completely renovated in 1989. The patterned beds are filled with 147 varieties of old-fashioned roses. Although the garden was bequeathed to the National Trust by Leonard Messel in 1954, his daughter and her husband (Lord and Lady Rosse) continued to further its development. The pinetum was virtually destroyed in the great storm of 1987, but it has now been replanted using over 150 varieties of conifers.

Gatehouse
Michelham Priory

On the banks of the Cuckmere River at Upper Dicker, near Hailsham, are the remains of an Augustinian priory founded in 1229 by Gilbert d'Aquila, Lord of the Rape of Pevensey. Surrounded by one of the largest moats in England, the property is entered through an impressive fourteenth-century, three-storeyed gatehouse. Much of the priory was destroyed at the Dissolution, including the church. The remaining monastic buildings, including the refectory, were incorporated into a Tudor house, and eventually a country mansion. The property is now owned by the Sussex Archaeological Society, who have restored many of the buildings, mounted exhibitions and events and laid out the grounds with spacious gardens. The watermill, fed by the moat, has been fully restored to working order. The sixteenth-century Great Barn, with its massive wooden beams, has doors of different heights, allowing carts to enter fully-laden through one side and leave empty through the other. Adjoining the barn is a museum celebrating the history of rope-making at Hailsham.

Bateman's

Nestling in the valley of the River Dudwell, south of the village of Burwash, the house called Bateman's was built by a Sussex ironmaster in 1634. Rudyard Kipling lived in the Jacobean property from 1902 until his death in 1936. It was here that he wrote such works as *Traffics and Discoveries* (1904), *Puck of Pook's Hill* (1906) and *Rewards and Fairies* (1910). Pook Hill lay to the south-west of the house, while 'the little mill that clacks, so busy by the brook', stood at the bottom of the garden. In 1903 Kipling installed a turbine- generator at the mill to provide the house with electricity. He and his American wife, Carrie, were also responsible for creating much of the garden, including a shallow pond for their children to sail boats or bathe in. One of the two 'fat-headed oasthouses with red-brick stomachs' is capped by a late nineteenth-century dovecote. Kipling was an early motoring enthusiast and his 1928 Rolls Royce can be found in the garage. Bateman's, with rooms laid out much as Kipling left them, now belongs to the National Trust.

Great Dixter

When Nathaniel Lloyd purchased the derelict fifteenth-century manor at Great Dixter in 1910, he commissioned the architect Edwin Lutyens to restore and extend the half-timbered building, which included the addition of a medieval hall house, moved from Benenden in Kent. Lutyens also designed the surrounding gardens, incorporating the old farm buildings and oasthouses into his overall plan. The planting, however, was undertaken by Nathaniel and his wife Daisy, who between them created one of the most exciting gardens in England with luxuriant informality complementing Lutyens' formal design. Today the gardens are looked after by Christopher Lloyd, the gardening writer, and feature a topiary depicting coffee-pots and peacocks, a wild meadow garden with rare flowers instead of a neatly trimmed lawn, a sunk garden with an octagonal pool and the Long Border, some 70 yards in length, where shrubs and small trees mingle with a wide variety of unusual plants. The house contains a fine collection of needlework and antique furniture.

Bayham Abbey

Lying in the valley of the River Teise, on the border of Kent and Sussex, Bayham Abbey was founded in about 1208 for Premonstratensian canons from the ailing houses of Otham, near Hailsham, and Brockley, near Lewisham. The monastery was suppressed in 1525 to raise money to pay for Cardinal Wolsey's proposed new colleges at Oxford. After Wolsey's fall, Bayham became the property of Henry VIII, who leased the estates to several of his friends, including Sir Anthony Browne, who also acquired Battle and Waverley Abbeys. At some time before 1752, when landscape began to be appreciated for its picturesque qualities, the landowner, John Pratt, erected a small Gothic-style villa on a site that would give the best view of the abbey ruins. Later in the century, the villa – now known as the Dower House – was enlarged by the second Lord Camden and the grounds landscaped by Humphry Repton. A mansion was built on the opposite side of the valley in 1870. The abbey, with its only surviving gatehouse across the border in Kent, is now in the care of English Heritage.

Mad Jack's Pyramid
Brightling

Scattered round the village of Brightling are a number of unusual objects and buildings. In the graveyard of the parish church, for example, is a 25-foot-high pyramid, built by Squire John Fuller as a mausoleum for himself in 1814. Legend holds that after his death in 1834 Fuller was buried sitting up, wearing top hat and tails and holding a bottle of claret. In fact he was buried beneath the floor of his folly in a recumbent position. A lifelong bachelor and MP for East Sussex, 'Mad Jack' acquired the land for his last resting place by agreeing to replace the inn, temptingly sited opposite the church, with a new one half-a-mile away. Having found that his boast of being able to see the spire of Dallington church from his house, Rose Hill, was untrue, Fuller saved face by building a similar spire – known as the Sugar Loaf – on the top of a nearby hill. His other Brightling follies include the Temple, the Observatory and the Tower. Construction of the four-mile wall surrounding his parkland was Fuller's way of relieving local unemployment.

Gatehouse
Battle Abbey

Some four years after his victory over the Anglo-Saxons at the battle of Senlac Hill, near Hastings, William I founded Battle Abbey as an act of atonement for the bloodshed of the Norman Conquest. Despite the unsuitability of the site – a narrow ridge sloping into marshland, with no natural water supply – William was adamant that the monastery should stand where the fighting had been fiercest, with the high altar of the abbey church marking the spot where King Harold died. In addition to endowing the abbey with six manors and the church at Cullompton in Devon, he granted the Benedictine monks certain privileges which included freedom from episcopal control: a right which oversucceeding centuries was systematically challenged by the Bishops of Chichester in whose see the monastery lay. During the French raids of the fourteenth century the monks helped to organize defences in the area between Pevensey and Romney. Abbey fortifications included the Great Gatehouse, built in 1338, and the wall-walk surrounding the precinct.

Reredorter and Dormitory
Battle Abbey

Battle Abbey was surrendered to Henry VIII on 27 May 1538 and the last abbot, John Hamond, was pensioned off with the substantial sum of £100 a year. Soon after, the monastery was granted to Sir Anthony Browne, who demolished the abbey church, chapter house and part of the cloisters, and converted the west range, including the abbot's house, into a mansion for himself. The monastic guest house was also rebuilt, reputedly as a royal residence for Prince Edward (later Edward VI) and Princess Elizabeth (later Elizabeth I), but there is no evidence that either of the children ever lived there. The abbey remained in the ownership of the Brownes until 1715, when the sixth Viscount Montague sold the estate to Sir Thomas Webster. Apart from an interval between 1857 and 1901, the abbey belonged to the Webster family until 1976, when it was purchased by the Department of the Environment. Browne's guest range was demolished in the mid-eighteenth century. The mansion was later improved and extended, and since the First World War has been occupied by Battle Abbey School.

CHICHESTER AND THE SUSSEX DOWNS

Belle Tout Lighthouse
near Birling Gap

In the early eighteenth century Jonathan Darby, the vicar of East Dean, excavated a cavern in the base of the chalk cliffs at Birling Gap, partly as a refuge for the shipwrecked and 'partly perhaps for himself, since Mrs Darby is said to have been gifted with unusual powers of loquacity.' (*Murray's Handbook for Travellers in Kent and Sussex*, 1858). Parson Darby's Hole, as it was called, has now disappeared through cliff erosion, but tradition maintains that it helped preserve the life of many shipwrecked sailors, guided to refuge and safety by a great lamp shining seaward from the cave. The Belle Tout lighthouse, on the cliff top above, was built to a design of Thomas Stevenson by 'Mad Jack' Fuller of Brightling in 1831, although it did not become operational until 1834. Despite a beam that could be seen over twenty miles away, the light was more often than not obscured by low cloud and mist. Eventually it was abandoned and replaced by a lighthouse at the foot of the cliffs at Beachy Head. The 46-foot-high Belle Tout is now a private residence.

In his autobiography, published in 1940, Eric Gill wrote of Chichester:

> The small modern growth of the town outside the walls was, forty years ago, almost negligible. Over more than half the length of the Roman wall (a great part of which is thick enough to form a broad footpath along the top) you could look straight out into green fields.

Although the city has now expanded beyond the ancient walls of Noviomagus, the main streets in the centre retain the pattern laid out by the Romans over 1,900 years ago. Excavations have revealed that the site of the former market was occupied during the Bronze Age, in about 1500 BC. Yet the earliest remains to survive above ground in the city are Roman – which also holds true for almost all of south-east England.

One of the first structures to be built by the invading legions was the supply-base at Richborough, near Sandwich, Kent, which subsequently became one of a chain of forts defending the Channel and North Sea coasts against Saxon raiders. Inside the grounds of Dover Castle are the unique remains of a first-century Roman *pharos*, or lighthouse, while in the town itself there is part of a well-preserved town house, with wall paintings, dating from the time when the port was the headquarters of the Roman Channel fleet. Perhaps the most exciting discovery of Roman occupation in the region was the palace at Fishbourne, near Chichester, with its decorative mosaics, underfloor heating systems and enclosed garden.

Architectural remains from the Dark Ages are sparse and mainly restricted to ecclesiastical buildings. One of the earliest is at Bargham, West Sussex, where flint foundations of an Anglo-Saxon church preserves brick fragments that are possibly Romano-British in origin. 'Whatever stood on top', Ian Nairn wrote in the Pevsner Buildings of England series, 'was almost certainly tall and narrow, a literal reaching up to God which still moves the visitor wherever it survives intact.' One of the most remarkable Anglo-Saxon structures to survive is the tower of St Mary's Church at Sompting, which has a unique 'Rhenish Helm', or gabled pyramidal cap. Harold Godwineson's historic visit to Normandy in 1064 was commemorated in the Bayeux Tapestry, which also depicted the future king entering the pre-Conquest church at Bosham, prior to his departure.

The arrival of William the Conqueror and his Norman followers, two years later, brought a new tradition of architecture to England – a style known on the Continent as Romanesque. A flurry of building activity followed. Almost every abbey church and cathedral was rebuilt on a grander and more ambitious scale: two of the most impressive being Chichester and Canterbury Cathedrals. In addition to founding numerous monasteries, including Battle Abbey on the spot where King Harold fell, the Normans erected strategically sited castles to protect their newly won territories: Eynsford, Rochester and Dover, for instance, with Arundel, Bramber and Lewes guarding gaps in the South Downs.

Further strongholds were built in the mid-fourteenth century because of the threat of French sea invasions. These included Amberley on the Arun and Bodiam on the Rother. The coastal forts of Walmer, Deal and Camber were constructed during the reign of Henry VIII. Upnor Castle dates from Elizabethan times, while the Martello Tower at Dymchurch was one link in a chain of similar strongholds erected because of the Napoleonic Wars in Europe.

Although there are several domestic dwellings with fragments dating from the eleventh century, most of the oldest surviving houses in the area are either thirteenth or fourteenth century. Remarkably, the rectory at Westdean, near Newhaven, has been inhabited for some seven hundred years. To discover a well-preserved medieval house in its original town or village setting is a surprisingly frequent occurrence. The Old Shop at Bignor, below the northern scarp of the South Downs, is one of the most famous. Dating from the fifteenth century, it displays many of the features of a traditional Wealden house, common throughout the South-East: timber-framing a central hall, and jettied upper storeys separated by wooden spandrels. Also typical of the region are the materials employed in its construction: brick nogging, both horizontal and herringbone, plus panels infilled with wattle and daub or with flints embedded in mortar. Instead of being tiled, however, as is more usual, the roof is thatched. With the addition of stone, plaster and, of course, wood, Nairn had good reason to call the mixture of textures 'captivating'.

The Weald and Downland Open Air Museum at Singleton preserves a fascinating variety of vernacular buildings from Kent, Surrey, Sussex and Hampshire. Where possible the museum promotes the retention of threatened buildings on their original site. But where there is no alternative, if money and space allow, properties are dismantled, moved and painstakingly reconstructed in the grounds of the museum. Here, without moving from the heart of the South Downs, visitors can experience much of the rich architectural heritage of the region, including a Wealden farmhouse from Chiddingstone, a weatherboarded barn from Cowfold, a medieval shop from Horsham, a flint cottage from

Hangleton and a saw-pit from Sheffield Park. In the woodland can be found a charcoal burner's hut, together with charcoal kilns in various stages of construction. Among the livestock on display are Southdown sheep and the local Sussex breed of cattle.

In addition to the more humble dwellings of town and country, there are countless manors and mansions. Many like Bateman's, Hatchlands, Petworth House, Ightham Mote and Polesden Lacey are now in the care of the National Trust. Others such as Belmont, Glynde Place, and Great Dixter House remain in private ownership. Yet, of all the region's buildings, perhaps the most audacious, and certainly the most celebrated, is the Royal Pavilion at Brighton, created in a style more resembling an Indian mogul's palace than the elegant Regency houses of the period.

Two prominent purpose-built structures, found scattered throughout the South-East (although many have been converted into private residences), are the windmill and the oasthouse. As the earliest written reference to a windmill in England concerns one at the manor of Iford, given to the monks of Lewes by Hugo de Plaiz in 1155, it is thought that windmills were invented earlier in the twelfth century. At first they were sited near the coast and on the Downs, with watermills continuing to provide the power to grind corn in the Weald. But with the growth of the Wealden woollen and iron industries, which needed the water to drive fulling- and hammer-mills, windmills began appear on suitable sites everywhere. Possibly the oldest to survive in Sussex is the post mill at High Salvington, dating from about 1720.

Although 'hoppehouses', specialized buildings for drying and packing hops, were recorded in the late sixteenth century, very few survive. The earliest type of kiln used for drying was rectangular. Gradually the buildings increased in size, and during the eighteenth century the characteristic, round oasthouse appeared – to be replaced by an improved rectangular type in the following century when the industry was at its peak. Modern developments in hop processing, however, indicate that, like windmills, all oast-houses will soon become redundant.

Whether windmill, mansion, castle or cathedral, buildings seldom fail to produce a response in the beholder, favourable or otherwise. Henry James wrote in 1879:

> The prettiest thing at Chichester is a charming little three-sided cloister, attached to the cathedral, where, as is usual in such places, you may sit upon a gravestone amid the deep grass in the middle and measure the great central mass of the church – the large gray sides, the high foundations of the spire, the parting of the nave and transept. From this point the greatness of a cathedral seems more complex and impressive. You watch the big shadows slowly change their relations; you listen to the cawing of rooks and the twittering of swallows; you hear a slow footstep echoing in the cloisters.

Lifeboat Station
Selsey Bill

The low-lying peninsula of Selsey Bill – eight miles south of Chichester – once extended more than a mile further out to sea. Offshore, somewhere under the waves, are the remains of Bishop (later Saint) Wilfrid's palace and the great Anglo-Saxon cathedral church he founded in 681. In the sixteenth century William Camden mentioned that the ruins were 'covered at high water, but plainly visible at low water.' Even today, the low cliffs at Selsey Bill are gradually slipping into the sea. The waters to the south of the peninsula are notorious for their dangerous currents and treacherous sandbanks. Over the years the lifeboat, launched from its station at the end of a catwalk, has saved many lives, including 120 passengers and crew on board the paddle-steamer *Queen*, which ran aground in 1908. Selsey derives its name from the Old English words meaning 'seal island'. Silting and the movement of shingle has now made it an integral part of the mainland. Pagham Harbour, on the eastern side of Selsey Bill, is a nature reserve attracting many rare birds.

Bosham

Sited on a small peninsula between two tidal creeks, four miles west of Chichester, the village of Bosham (pronounced 'Bozzam') was an important port in Anglo-Saxon and medieval times. Legend says that it was here (or at Southampton) that Canute (or Cnut) failed to halt the advance of the incoming tide. Although the king's connection with Bosham is much-disputed, it is thought that his young daughter was buried in the church (her alleged remains were discovered inside a stone coffin in 1865). Bosham also lays claim to being the oldest site of Christianity in Sussex, for there was a small community of Irish monks here long before St Wilfrid's missionary visit in 681. In 1064 Harold Godwineson, Earl of Wessex (soon to become the last Anglo-Saxon King of England), embarked from Bosham harbour to visit Normandy. His departure and his ill-fated oath of allegiance to Duke William were depicted in the Bayeux Tapestry, as was also Bosham church, which, though altered, still retains much of the Anglo-Saxon building.

Chichester Cathedral

The origins of Chichester Cathedral lie submerged under the sea at Selsey Bill, eight miles south, where, it is said, the bells of the first cathedral church, founded there in the late seventh century, can sometimes be heard. In 1075, after the Norman Conquest, the see was transferred to Chichester. The present building, standing on the site of an Anglo-Saxon church, dates from the time of Bishop Ralph de Luffa, who succeeded to the see in 1091. Although the cathedral was badly damaged by fire in 1114 and also in 1187, building (or rebuilding) continued throughout the succeeding centuries. Both tower and spire collapsed in 1861 but were rebuilt. The detached bell-tower, near the north porch, is the only one to survive in an English cathedral. Chichester dates back at least to Roman times, when the fortified town of Noviomagus, or 'new market', was established with a temple dedicated to Neptune and Minerva. The Roman plan of four main streets meeting at the centre remains, except that at their intersection there now stands a crown-like Market Cross, dating from 1501.

Roman Palace
Fishbourne

Excavation in the 1960s at Fishbourne, just over a mile west of Chichester, revealed the remains of a palace which proved to be one of the largest and most important Roman residences in Britain. Built on the site of a Roman military supply base, which was occupied shortly after Emperor Claudius's invasion of south-east England in AD 43, the vast palace complex dates from about AD 75 and may have been the residence of Tiberius Claudius Cogidubnus, who adopted the name of his patron, the Emperor, and was client-king of the Chichester-based Regni tribe. Although the site has only been partly excavated, the visible remains – now roofed over – include such ground-level features as tessellated pavements, underfloor heating systems (hypocausts) and decorative mosaics. The northern half of the formal garden has been laid out exactly on its original plan with trees, plants and shrubs favoured by the Romans. It seems that boats could sail right up to the terrace edge, south of the garden, by means of a dredged channel linked to a large, shallow, seawater lagoon.

Guest House
Boxgrove Priory

Founded for Benedictine monks during the reign of Henry I (1100-35), Boxgrove Priory was originally a cell of Lessay Abbey in Normandy. It was granted its independence in the fourteenth century during the Hundred Years' War. Although many of the monastic buildings were demolished after the Dissolution, the remains today include the roofless Guest House, dating from about 1300, and a fragment of the Norman Chapter House. The whole west part of the priory church, including most of the nave, was destroyed, but the Norman tower and transepts and Early English chancel were saved to become the parish church. The entwined heraldry and foliage decoration on the vaulted chancel ceiling was painted by Lambert Bernard in the sixteenth century. At roughly the same time, in 1532, Lord Thomas de la Warr built the Chantry Chapel. Records state that in 1622 two churchwardens were reprimanded for encouraging children to play cricket in the churchyard, where windows could get broken and 'a little child had like to have her brains beaten out with a cricket bat'.

Halnaker Mill

A prominent landmark on the summit of Halnaker Hill, five miles north-east of Chichester, this brick tower windmill, built in about 1750, was a ruin when Hilaire Belloc wrote his poem *Ha'nacker Mill* in 1912, therein likening its condition to the deterioration of agriculture in England. Restored externally in 1934 as a memorial to the wife of Sir William Bird, it is an empty shell with bricked-up windows. At the foot of the hill in the grounds of Little Halnaker, built in 1961, are the remains of Halnaker House, begun by Robert de Haye in the twelfth century and remodelled by Lord Thomas de la Warr in the sixteenth century. It fell into ruin in about 1800 when its owner, the third Duke of Richmond, rebuilt his house at Goodwood a mile or so to the west. On the top of the downs, in 1801, the Duke also laid out a racecourse, which is now world-famous for its 'Glorious Goodwood' meeting in July. On St Roche's Hill, overlooking the racecourse, are the earth-work remains of a Neolithic causewayed camp and also an Iron Age hill-fort, known as the Trundle.

Singleton
from the Trundle

Nestling in the valley of the River Lavant, in the heart of the South Downs, this compact village, with its flint and brick cottages, has a church dating back to Anglo-Saxon times. After the opening of nearby Goodwood racecourse in 1801 Singleton rose in prominence. Even the Prince of Wales (later Edward VII) stabled his horses in the village. Cobbett visited the area in August 1823 and wrote: 'I saw, and with great delight, a pig at almost every labourer's house. The houses are good and warm; and the gardens some of the very best that I have seen in England.' On the outskirts of Singleton is the Weald and Downland Open Air Museum, founded in 1967 by J.R. Armstrong to preserve examples of vernacular buildings that would otherwise have been demolished. Among the Sussex buildings reconstructed on the museum site are the elementary School from West Wittering, the Watermill from Lurgashall, Pendean farmhouse from Midhurst and the Granary from Littlehampton. From the summit of the Trundle Iron Age hill-fort there are extensive views in all directions.

Market Hall
Weald and Downland Open Air Museum

Originally built at Titchfield, Hampshire, in the sixteenth and early seventeenth centuries, the Market Hall – standing on timber posts – was dismantled and reconstructed at the Weald and Downland Open Air Museum as part of a typical medieval market place. The entrance at the side leads up to a first-floor chamber, traditionally used by the town council. The space under the stairs served as a temporary lock-up or 'cage' for trouble-makers, while the open, but covered, arcade at street level was used by market traders. The Medieval Shop (on the left of the photograph) came from Horsham, West Sussex. Dating from the late fifteenth century, the timber-framed building is divided into two separate shops. Access to the upper floors is by way of a staircase at the rear of only one of the shops. The Upper Hall (on the right of the photograph) was brought from Crawley, West Sussex, where it was used as a store shed, known as 'the old barn'. The upper hall is now used as a meeting room, while the ground floor houses the museum's library.

The Old Shop
Bignor

Close by Stane Street, the
straight Roman highway that
ran from Chichester to London,
is the small downland village
of Bignor, with its houses,
cottages and church laid out
in a rectangle of narrow lanes.
The Old Shop, now a private
residence, is a celebrated
example of a fifteenth-century
Wealden house, with thatched
roof, jettied upper storeys and
timber-framing, infilled with
a variety of materials including
brick and flint. The parish
church of Holy Cross, essentially
thirteenth century, contains
a Norman chancel arch. On
18 July 1811, whilst ploughing
in the fields east of the village,
George Tupper struck a large
stone and discovered the remains
of a Roman villa, which after
excavation proved to be one of
the largest in Britain, covering
some four-and-a-half acres.
Among the intricate mosaic
floors, dating mainly from
the fourth century, are
representations of Venus
and the Gladiators, the Four
Seasons, the Head of Medusa
and Ganymede being carried
aloft by an eagle. On Bignor Hill
are the earthwork remains of a
Neolithic causewayed camp.

St John's Church
Bury

On downland slopes at the
northern end of the Arun
gap, some five miles north of
Arundel, this ancient village with
its crossroads and pond contains
an attractive collection of
Wealden houses and cottages,
many of which are built of
sandstone. At the eastern end
of the village, beside the River
Arun, is the twelfth-century
church of St John the Evangelist,
standing on the site of an earlier
foundation mentioned in the
Domesday Book of 1086. The
shingled broach-spire was added
to the thirteenth-century tower
in about 1600. At the opposite
end of the village is Bury House
the country home of John
Galsworthy (1867-1933), author
of *The Forsyte Saga* (1922), who
purchased the property in 1920.
Although he died at Hampstead,
his ashes were scattered
on the downs above Bury.
Nairn considered 'Fogdens',
constructed in the Kentish style
of timber-framing, to be the
best cottage in the village. Other
buildings of interest include the
nineteenth-century post office,
with eccentric stone carvings,
and the seventeenth-century
Bury Manor.

Amberley

Standing on elevated ground at the foot of the South Downs escarpment and at the northern end of the Arun gap, Amberley, with its church, castle, winding streets and cottages, is considered by many to be the perfect Sussex village. Although, architecturally, none of the cottages are particularly remarkable on their own, as a whole they are romantically appealing. All are uniquely different and employ a variety of building materials – thatch, stone, brick, flint, timber and tile. The castle, or fortified manor house, was built in the late fourteenth century by Bishop William Rede as a defence against French raiders and incorporates the earlier residence of the Bishops of Chichester. Partly a ruin, it is now a country hotel. St Michael's Church, just outside the castle walls, dates from shortly after the Norman Conquest. Amberley Chalk Pits Museum, set in a disused chalk quarry near the railway station, contains exhibits illustrating the industrial history of the South-East. To the north, the water-meadows of Amberley Wild Brooks are a haven for wildlife.

St Mary's Church
Climping

An old West Sussex saying about churches goes: 'Bosham for antiquity, Boxgrove for beauty, but Climping for perfection.' Indeed, St Mary's at Climping is considered to be one of the finest, unaltered Early English churches in the region. Standing on the coastal plain a mile inland from Climping Sands – west of Littlehampton – it was built in about 1220, probably by John de Clymping (later Bishop of Chichester). The stone was imported from Caen in Normandy. Incorporated in the building is the lower part of the massive Norman tower of about 1170. The pointed lancet window on the first floor, with zigzag moulding all the way round, is considered to be unique in England, as may also be the west doorway, with its trefoiled inner arch, chevron columns, and dog-tooth and zigzag moulding. On either side of the doorway is a plain narrow vertical niche the left one surmounted by a roundel and the right by a lozenge. Cut into the wall near the latter are two crosses said to have been made by a Crusader, possibly Savaric III de Bohun, prior to his departure for the Holy Land in 1190.

Arundel

The skyline of the ancient town of Arundel, situated on a long ridge sloping down to the banks of the River Arun, is dominated by a castle, a church and a cathedral. The castle, ancestral home of the Dukes of Norfolk, is open to the public and contains a fine collection of paintings and furniture. At Burpham, on the opposite site of the Arun valley, are the earthwork remains of a second castle, about which little is known except that it was in use during Danish times. The church, St Nicholas's, is uniquely both Church of England and Roman Catholic. It dates from the late fourteenth century and is, according to Nairn, 'a good harmonious example of what the Early Perpendicular style meant in South East England'. The Fitzalan Chapel, originally in the collegiate part of the church, can now only be entered through the castle grounds. The Roman Catholic cathedral of Our Lady and St Philip Howard (formerly dedicated to St Philip Neri) was built in 1869-73 by the fifteenth Duke and designed by J. A. Hansom in the French Gothic style of about 1400.

Chanctonbury Ring

On the downs above the village of Washington, are the earthwork remains of a small Iron Age hill-fort, known as Chanctonbury Ring. Its 780-foot-high summit is crowned by a distinctive clump of beech trees, planted in 1760 by the young Charles Goring of nearby Wiston Park. Reputedly, he nurtured the seedlings for months, carrying bottles of water up the hill until they were firmly established. Shortly before his death, at the age of eighty-five, he wrote a poem thanking God that he had lived to see the Ring 'in all its beauty dress'd'. Amidst the trees beneath the thin downland soil are the foundations of two Romano-British buildings, one of which was a temple. Local tradition (thought to be derived from an ancient ritual dance once celebrated on the hill) says that the Devil will appear to anyone who runs seven times round the Ring on a dark night. A few hundred yards west of the Ring beside the South Downs Way is a 'dew pond', made to hold drinking water for sheep. The photograph was taken from the Ring looking east towards Wiston Park and Steyning.

Cissbury Ring

On the chalk downs above Worthing are the remains of Neolithic flint mines, some of which were over 40 feet deep, with horizontal galleries radiating from the floor of the central shaft. Dug with tools like antler picks and ox shoulder-blade shovels, the miners, who used lamps, chose to work the best-quality seams, even if it meant that they had to dig deeper. The mines at Cissbury, near Findon, were worked over 4000 years ago, at roughly the same time as those on Blackpatch Hill and Harrow Hill, both to the north-west. The oval-shaped Iron Age hill-fort of Cissbury Ring, which encroaches on the flint-mine site, was erected in about 250 BC and encloses an area of some 65 acres. During Romano-British times the interior came under the plough, and in the early fourth century the massive outer defences were refortified, possibly against Saxon raiders. The views from the 603-foot-high hill are extensive, embracing the tree-crowned landmark of Chanctonbury Ring to the north, Beachy Head to the south-east and the Isle of Wight to the south-west.

St Mary's Church
Sompting

On a prominent hill-top site north-east of Worthing, the parish church of St Mary at Sompting has the only remaining Anglo-Saxon tower in England with a gabled pyramidal cap, known as a 'Rhenish Helm', a style more commonly found along the Rhine and in Germany. The church – except for the tower – was rebuilt by the Knights Templar in the latter half of the twelfth century. Inside, supporting the tower, is an off-centre, crudely carved Anglo-Saxon arch, seemingly influenced by classical Roman design. In the early fourteenth century, after the dissolution of the Knights Templar, the church was granted to the Knights of St John, or Knights Hospitaller, who built a chapel on the north side of the tower and nave. The modern building inside the chapel ruins was erected in 1971. Although the Order of St John was suppressed in England in 1540, it was revived in 1877 as the St John Ambulance Association, and aptly they were presented with the Patronage of St Mary's church in 1963. The south porch was probably added in the late fifteenth century.

Post Mill
High Salvington

The black weather-boarded post
mill at High Salvington, three
miles north of Worthing pier,
dates from about 1720 and
ceased working in 1897. The
long, painstaking process of
restoration to full working order
began in 1976. Contrary to
popular belief, the main centre-
post – about which the upper
body of the mill can turn to face
the wind – is not the trunk of
a growing tree with roots. In
the round base of the mill is a
small house, now used to serve
refreshments to visitors. The
ladder, which gives access to
the upper floor, is hinged at the
top so that it can be lifted clear
of the ground when the mill is
turned. This was done by moving
the wheeled tailpole, usually by
man-power, but sometimes by
harnessing it to a horse. The
compass-type tailpole on High
Salvington mill is the only one
to survive in Sussex. Windmills
were once a common feature
of the South Downs, especially
during the eighteenth and
nineteenth centuries when
sheep-rearing declined in favour
of arable farming. Although they
were mainly used to grind corn,
some were employed to pump
water.

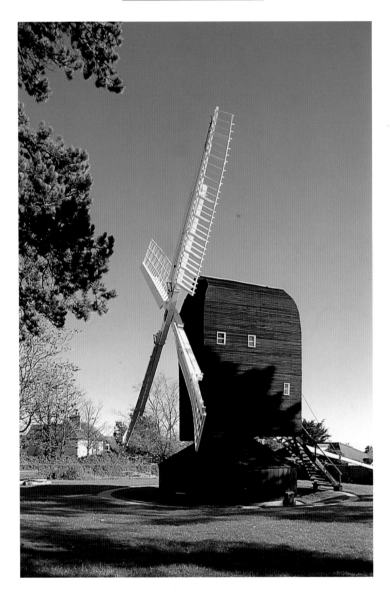

St Mary's House
Bramber

On the west bank of the River
Adur, east of Steyning, the
ancient borough of Bramber
is now little more than a single
short street with the church and
castle ruins at one end and the
timber-framed building called
St Mary's House at the other.
During medieval times it was
a small market town and inland
port, ceasing to be the latter
when the river silted up in
the thirteenth century. Defoe,
writing in 1724-5, said that it
'hardly deserves the name of a
town, having not above fifteen
or sixteen families in it, and of
them not many above asking
you for alms as you ride by'.
He also added that the elections
(in which two members were
sent to Parliament) were
'scandalously mercenary.'
St Mary's was built in about
1470 as a dwelling for bridge
wardens, who were Benedictine
monks from Sele Priory at Upper
Beeding, across the river. It also
served as a hostel for pilgrims
and travellers. Local tradition,
not supported by the facts,
claims that Charles II, fleeing
from the battle of Worcester
in 1651, spent his last night
in England at the house before
embarking from Shoreham
for France.

Church Street
Steyning

Situated at the foot of the South Downs escarpment, at the meeting-point of several roads, Steyning was an established settlement with two churches, four mills and borough status when the Domesday Book was compiled in 1086. In medieval times it was a small market town, connected to the sea, like Bramber, by a quay on the River Adur. The Norman church of St Andrew at Steyning stands on the site of a wooden church built by St Cuthman in the eighth century. For a time the town was known as St Cuthman's Port. According to Nairn, the houses on the south side of Church Street 'have just the right sort of variation within a common rhythm'. Ranging in date from the fifteenth to the seventeenth century, the properties employ a pleasing mixture of building materials, including timber-framing, brick, plaster, stone, flint, cobbles and tiles. The Old Grammar School (in the left of the photograph) was founded in 1614 and incorporates the long timber-framed range of a fifteenth-century guildhall, with a first-floor overhang. In the centre is a brick porch, heightened in the nineteenth century.

The Old Cottage
North Lancing

Many of the older buildings in south-east England were constructed from materials found in the immediate locality. The Old Cottage at North Lancing dates from the fifteenth century. Its timber-framing employs the style known as 'Kentish framing', where a jettied front window is set centrally between a pair of downward curving braces. Although oak was the most commonly used timber, elm – despite being less able to resist woodworm and the effects of weather – was the dominant hardwood on the coastal plain of Sussex. As corn was the area's predominant crop, thatch became the characteristic roof covering. Bricks, which became popular in the region from the sixteenth century, were often used to infill the timber-framing. Plastering over the infill material, especially if it was wattle and daub, provided protection against the elements. Perhaps the most famous building in Lancing is the college, founded in 1848 by Nathaniel Woodard. Built of flint and locally quarried stone, the public school and chapel stand high up on a spur of the downs overlooking the valley of the Adur.

Smock Mill
West Blatchington

Standing on top of a square
flint tower and forming part of
a barn complex, the smock mill
at West Blatchington, built in
about 1820, strangely resembles
a church with sails. It was
painted by Constable in
1825 and originally stood in a
farmyard. Today it is completely
surrounded by houses. The
mill is unusual in that its timber
body, or smock, is hexagonal.
Although countless watermills
were recorded in the Domesday
Book of 1086, the earliest
written reference to a windmill
in England is dated 1155. This
and the record of a windmill
at Bishopstone, East Sussex, in
1191 seem to suggest that they
were invented earlier in the
twelfth century. Before steam
power made them redundant,
map-makers recorded some
15,000 windmill sites in Britain;
many more, no doubt, existed,
but had been destroyed. There
are three types of windmill:
the post mill, the tower mill and
the smock mill, the last possibly
appearing towards the end of
the seventeenth century. Smock
mills are similar to tower mills,
except that their bodies are clad
with weather-boarding.

Royal Pavilion
Brighton

The small fishing port of
Brighthelmstone (later shortened
to Brighton) was transformed
into one of the most fashionable
resorts in England after a visit
in 1783 by the Prince of Wales
(Prince Regent from 1811 and
George IV from 1820). His
stay was prompted by the fame
of Dr Richard Russell, a local
physician, who published a
book in the 1750s extolling
the beneficial effect of seawater
in 'diseases of the glands'. The
Royal Pavilion stands on the site
of a small farmhouse leased by
the prince in 1786. Over the
following year he had the
architect, Henry Holland,
rebuild it as a classical villa
with a central rotunda and
dome. Further rebuilding
and enlargement, culminating
with the work of John Nash in
1815-22, produced one of the
most celebrated architectural
fantasies in Europe, with Indian
style domes, pinnacles and
minarets. The spectacularly
inventive Chinese decoration
and furniture of the interior are
credited to the combined efforts
of George IV, Nash, the designers
Frederick Crace and Robert
Jones, and the artist Lambelet.

Palace Pier
Brighton

Recorded in the Domesday Book as Bristelmestune, a name derived from 'Beorhthelm's (or Bright Helmet's) enclosure', the settlement at Brighton – built on the foreshore beneath the cliffs – was described by Defoe in about 1724 as 'a poor fishing town'. He also mentioned that the inhabitants were trying 'to beg money all over England, to raise banks against the water', which had already devoured over 100 houses and, if left unchecked, would end up destroying the whole town. Subsequent protective measures proved ineffective and the settlement moved from the foreshore to the top of the cliffs. Erosion still continued, however, and in 1803 the first stretch of concrete sea-wall was built. Groynes, first of wood and later of concrete, helped stem the movement of shingle. Britain's first electric railway was constructed by Magnus Volk to run along Brighton's seafront in 1883. There are two piers: the 600-yard-long Palace Pier, opened in 1901, and the West Pier, opened in 1866 but now closed to the public. The huge marina was opened in 1979.

Harbour Breakwater
Newhaven

Rising in the heart of the Weald, near St Leonards Forest, the Ouse curves in a south-easterly direction to Lewes, before entering the sea at Newhaven. The original mouth of the river was at Seaford, but in 1579 a freak storm diverted the course of the Ouse westward to Meeching. Seaford ceased to be a port and Meeching became Newhaven. To prevent the harbour silting up a 3000-foot-long breakwater was begun in 1880 and completed in 1891. King Louis Philippe of France stayed in the Bridge Hotel (now Bridge Inn) after fleeing the revolution of 1848. Apparently, he booked in with Queen Marie Amelie under the names 'Mr and Mrs Smith'. Newhaven Fort, overlooking the harbour, was built by Lord Palmerston in 1864-71. The main traffic of the port is cross-Channel, with a ferry service to and from Dieppe. In his *Highways and Byways in Sussex* (1912) E.V. Lucas wrote: 'Of Newhaven there is little to say, except that in rough weather the traveller from France is very glad to reach it, and on a fine day the traveller from England is happy to leave it behind.'

Front Entrance
Glynde Place

Glynde Place was built of chalk blocks, Caen stone and Sussex flint for the ironmaster, William Morley, in 1579. Richard Trevor, later Bishop of Durham, rebuilt the property in the 1750s, changing the main entrance to the east front, and creating a new approach through the eighteenth-century stable block to the south. He also built the Palladian-style parish church of St Mary in 1763-5. In the churchyard is the grave of John Ellman (1753-1832), the sheep-breeder who established the Southdown sheep. One mile north, at Glyndebourne, is the famous opera house, founded by John Christie (1882-1952) in the garden of his home. Each year, since 1934, it has been the venue for a summer season of international opera, for which the audience (or promenaders) wear evening dress and bring picnics to be consumed during the interval. A new and larger opera house, designed by Michael Hopkins, opened in 1994. Charleston Farmhouse, some two miles south-east of Glynde Place, was the home of Duncan Grant and Clive and Vanessa Bell, members of the Bloomsbury Group, who began to meet in London about 1906.

South Downs
from Ditchling Beacon

At 813 feet above sea-level, Ditchling Beacon is the third highest point on the South Downs, and as such offers magnificent views across the Sussex Weald. Near the Beacon, which is owned by the National Trust, are the earthwork remains of an Iron Age hill-fort and, to the west, a couple of 'dew ponds', created in the eighteenth and nineteenth centuries for watering sheep. The South Downs Way, stretching for 99 miles between Eastbourne and Winchester, passes along the crest of the downland ridge. The crossroads village of Ditchling, below, with its ancient church, green and duck pond, contains a sixteenth-century, timber-framed house, known as Wings Place or, sometimes, Anne of Cleves House, because the land was granted to Henry VIII's fourth wife as part of her divorce settlement. Since the early nineteenth century the village has been the home of artists and craftsmen, including Frank Brangwyn (1867-1956), the painter, and Eric Gill (1882-1940), the sculptor, typographer and writer. Some of their works are on display in Ditchling Museum.

Lewes Castle

One of a chain of fortifications guarding gaps in the South Downs, Lewes Castle was built shortly after the Norman Conquest by William de Warenne, who became the first Earl of Surrey in about 1087. Standing on a dominant site overlooking the River Ouse, the stronghold eventually had two artificial mounds, one at each end of a long, oval bailey. Both mounds were crowned with shell keeps, but only the south-western keep, erected by the early twelfth century, survives. It was strengthened with two polygonal towers in the thirteenth century. The mighty barbican, or outer gateway, was built in the early fourteenth century. The battlemented Castle Lodge dates from about 1860. At Southover, just south of the town, William de Warenne and his wife, Gundrada, founded the Cluniac priory of St Pancras, which subsequently became the chief house of the Order in England. The buildings were demolished at the Dissolution and all that now remains are ruins. North-west of the town, on 14 May 1264, the Royalist army of Henry III and Prince Edward was defeated by Simon de Montfort.and the Barons.

Anne of Cleves House
Lewes

As part of her divorce settlement, the fourth wife of Henry VIII, Anne of Cleves, was granted property in Sussex, including the manor of Southover, which contained the tile-hung, timber-framed Wealden house inappropriately named after her at Lewes. Built above a medieval tunnel-vaulted cellar in about 1530, the house originally belonged to the nearby Priory of St Pancras. The front porch bears the date 1599 and also the initials of John Saxpes, who was probably responsible for adding the two-transomed hall window and the three-storeyed Elizabethan west wing. Today the property houses a museum of local history, with displays ranging from Wealden ironwork to Sussex pottery. Among the many other buildings of interest in the ancient market town of Lewes is Bull House, the home, from 1768 to 1774, of Thomas Paine, the left-wing politician and writer who was active in the American and French Revolutions.

Parish Church
Southease

On the west bank of the River Ouse, overlooking a sloping village green, the parish church at Southease is one of only three in Sussex with a Norman round tower (the others being St John's at Piddinghoe and St Michael's at Lewes). In 1966 the little flint church celebrated a thousand years of recorded history, marking the charter signed by Edgar, King of the English, in 966, when he granted both church and manor to Hyde Abbey at Winchester. The church building, which dates from the early twelfth century, remained the property of the monastery until the Reformation. In 1934-5 thirteenth-century wall paintings were revealed which once covered the whole of the interior. In 1604 the church register recorded the marriage of a widower, adding in Latin: 'A shipwrecked sailor seeks a second shipwreck.' From Southease a cul-de-sac leads to Telscombe, once a centre for training racehorses. Set in a downland hollow, much of the village was bequeathed to Brighton Borough Council in 1933. Monk's House at nearby Rodmell was the country home of Leonard and Virginia Woolf from 1919 to 1969.

Firle Beacon

From the 712-foot-high summit of Firle Beacon there are extensive views over the South Downs, the Channel and the Weald. The round tower (visible in the distance in the photograph) was built in 1819 by the fourth Viscount Gage of Firle Place for his gamekeeper, who could survey the estate from the top and signal by waving flags. It is said that when the viscount returned home by train, his manservant signalled from the carriage window by waving a white handkerchief. The message would be relayed to the house by means of a flag on the tower, and by the time the viscount arrived at the railway station a carriage would be waiting. By means of the flags and a telescope the gamekeeper could also communicate with the keepers at Plashett Park, five miles north. Tradition also says that the greengage was named after the botanical traveller Thomas Gage, who brought a specimen home and planted it in his garden, thereby introducing it into the country. Firle Place, the ancestral home of the Gage family, is regularly open to the public and contains a fine collection of paintings and furniture.

The Long Man of Wilmington

The Long Man of Wilmington is one of only two giant figures to survive in Britain. Like the Cerne Abbas Giant his outline is carved in the green turf of a chalk hill, but there any similarity ends. Sometimes called the Lanky Man or the Lone Man, the tall enigmatic figure stands on the steep escarpment of Windover Hill facing the village of Wilmington. His present appearance dates from 1874, and is based on a shadowy and indistinct figure noticed by Dr J.S. Phené the previous year. Now outlined with white concrete blocks, the Long Man is over 231 feet tall. The staff in his left hand is 241 feet long, while the one in his right is four feet shorter. They are 115 feet apart. From a rough, and probably unreliable, sketch made by Sir William Burrell in 1779, it appears that the giant in his earlier form held a rake in his right hand and a scythe in his left. Tradition says that he also wore a hat, or possibly a helmet. But this confusion is thought to have arisen from the local weather rhyme:

> When Firle Hill and Long Man
> has a cap,
> We in the valley gets a drap.

Clergy House
Alfriston

The first building to be purchased by the National Trust after its foundation in 1895 was the timber-framed Wealden house at Alfriston on the west bank of the Cuckmere River. Dating from the mid-fourteenth century, the property – which has a central hall rising to the rafters – was probably built by a yeoman farmer, before being acquired by Michelham Priory in 1400. Surrounded by a small cottage garden, the Clergy House stands on the village green, called the Tye, near the cruciform church of St Andrew, known as the Cathedral of the Downs because of its size. Before the river silted up, the village was a port and busy market centre. The old market cross, although badly damaged, still stands in the triangular village square. During the early nineteenth century most of the population were involved in smuggling. The Market Inn (or Ye Olde Smugglers Inne) was the headquarters of the Alfriston Gang, led by Stanton Collins. The Star Inn, once a medieval pilgrims' hospice, is noted for its red-painted ship's figurehead and colourful carvings.

White Horse
Hindover Hill

Not far from the famous Long Man of Wilmington is another carved figure, a white horse, visible from the Cuckmere Valley and the South Downs Way. Known as the Litlington Horse, it is, in fact, one of two horses that stood on the steep side of Hindover, or High and Over, Hill. The earlier figure, said to have been carved in a day to commemorate the coronation of Queen Victoria in 1838, has now vanished and its exact position can no longer be identified. All that is known is that it stood about 100 yards north-west of the present horse, which dates from the 1920s and is 88 feet long and 66 feet high. In *White Horses and Other Hill Figures* (1949) Morris Marples wrote:

> Below the horse is a large letter S, and to its right an irregular shape, roughly resembling a lion's head and now considerably overgrown; whether this ever represented anything or had any connection with the horse is not known locally.... It is strange how quickly such things are forgotten.

Like many other hill figures, it was camouflaged during the Second World War.

All Saints Church and Parsonage
Westdean

Nestling in a fold of the South Downs, at the western edge of Friston Forest, the sheltered and secluded hamlet of Westdean contains a flint and stone church, an ancient parsonage and the ruins of a medieval manor house, possibly occupying the site of the palace of Alfred the Great mentioned by the ninth-century chronicler Asser. The parish church of All Saints, with its Norman and fourteenth-century bell tower capped by a squat, gabled spire, contains several interesting memorials including one to Mrs Susanna Tirrey (d. 1637), which Pevsner called 'decidedly funny'. The church also contains two bronze heads: one of the painter Sir Oswald Birley (1880-1952), by Clare Sheridan, and the other of the statesman Lord Waverley (d.1958), by Jacob Epstein. The Old Parsonage House nearby, with walls over two feet thick, dates from about 1280 and is claimed to be one of the oldest inhabited small houses in the country. The original building was sympathetically extended in 1894. Within the high flint walls of the former manor house are the roofless remains of a circular medieval dovecote.

Cuckmere Valley
from Cradle Hill

Rising in the heart of the Sussex Weald, the Cuckmere River flows southward past Hailsham, Michelham Priory, Alfriston, Litlington and Exceat, before debouching into the Channel at Cuckmere Haven. The photograph was taken looking east across one of the river's impressive meanders towards Charleston Bottom and the dark woodland of Friston Forest. In the churchyard at Friston – entered by a 'tapsel' gate, pivoting on a vertical axis – are the gravestones of several unknown seamen. One, a simple wooden cross, bears the poignant words: 'WASHED ASHORE'. Lullington Heath Nature Reserve, to the north of the forest, supports an astonishing mix of plants, with species that thrive on chalk downland growing side by side with varieties that prefer acid heathland. The church at Lullington, on the road between Litlington and Wilmington, is noted for being the smallest church in Sussex, despite the fact that it is the restored chancel of a much larger church. About sixteen feet square, it has a white weather-boarded bell turret and is still used for regular worship.

Seven Sisters
from Short Cliff

The South Downs meet the sea at Beachy Head and the Seven Sisters – a line of perpendicular white cliffs stretching from a point south-west of Eastbourne to Cuckmere Haven. Although the undulating cliff top between Birling Gap and Cliff End has long been known as the Seven Sisters, the number of ridges, in fact, total eight: Haven Brow, Short Brow, Rough Brow, Brass Point, Flagstaff Point, Flat Hill, Baily's Brow and Went Hill Brow. The seven troughs – which some claim to be the Sisters – are the heads of truncated valleys and, like the ridges, have been shorn-off by the erosive action of the sea. In ancient times the valleys were cut by rivers, but today they hang high and dry many feet above the shore. It is estimated that, unprotected, the cliffs recede at an average rate of around two to three feet a year. Cliff falls are common, especially during a severe winter when the soft and friable chalk readily succumbs to shattering by frost. The 692-acre Seven Sisters Country Park at Exceat includes a part of the Seven Sisters and Cuckmere Valley.

Lighthouse
Beachy Head

Rising sheer from the sea to 534 feet, the chalk cliff of Beachy Head is the highest on the south coast and has been designated an Area of Outstanding Natural Beauty and a Site of Special Scientific Interest. Lying to the south-west of Eastbourne, the *Beauchef,* or 'fair head', as the Normans called it, is one of the most famous landmarks in England. The distinctive red-and-white lighthouse at the foot of the headland was erected in 1902. Despite appearing like a tiny replica model, it stands 142 feet high and casts a powerful beam that can be seen for 25 miles. In *Hours of Spring,* published in 1886, Richard Jefferies wrote of a walk up the hill from Eastbourne:

> Every step crumbled up numbers of minute grey shells, empty and dry, that crunched underfoot like hoar-frost or fragile beads. They were very pretty; it was a shame to crush them. They lay in millions in the depths of the sward, and I thought as I broke them unwillingly that each of these had once been a house of life. A living creature dwelt in each and felt the joy of existence.

Pier and Seafront
Eastbourne

Lying at the eastern foot of the South Downs east of Beachy Head, Eastbourne, although an ancient settlement, owes its main expansion as a seaside resort to William Cavendish, Earl of Burlington (later seventh Duke of Devonshire), who encouraged its development on his estate in 1851. The pier, some 1,000 feet long, was designed by Eugenius Birch. Work began in 1866 and, despite being unfinished, it was officially opened in 1870. The shoreward section was swept away in a storm in 1877 and rebuilt at a higher level, hence the ramp partway along the pier. By retaining the shifting shingle the wooden groynes help protect the three-mile seafront from the fury of the waves. Positioned along the front are several small forts, which were built as a defence against Napoleonic invasion and include the Redoubt, erected between 1804 and 1812, and the Wish Tower, a restored Martello Tower (no.73 out of a total of 74 between Seaford and Folkestone). Both contain small museums. As one of the region's premier holiday resorts, the town offers a wide variety of attractions and events.

DOVER AND THE CINQUE PORTS

Fairfield Church

Before the marsh was effectively drained the church of St Thomas Becket at Fairfield – standing in lonely isolation amidst sheep-grazed pastureland – was accessible for most of the year only by boat or on horseback. According to legend it was built by an unnamed Archbishop of Canterbury who was riding across the marsh when he accidentally fell into a dyke. Having been rescued from drowning by a farmer, he gave thanks by erecting the church and dedicating it to his martyred predecessor. Although the date of its foundation is uncertain, a timber-framed church is known to have existed on the site in the thirteenth century. In 1912 the building was dismantled, given new timbers where necessary and painstakingly reconstructed, with the addition of an outer fabric of red and blue brick. The church of St Augustine at Brookland, two miles east, is noted for its unusual detached wooden belfry. Some 60 feet high, it is thought to date from the late twelfth or thirteenth century and consists of three octagonal cones stacked one on top of the other.

Some 7,000 years ago, when the sea broke through the land bridge between Britain and the rest of Europe, the south-east coast of England became both the gateway and the bulwark of the island. At its closest point England is only 21 miles from France and has, therefore, always been vulnerable to invasion. During prehistoric times thriving cross-Channel trade routes were established by successive waves of migratory settlers, culminating in the Celts, or Britons, to whom Gaius Julius Caesar turned his attention in the first century BC. While in the process of consolidating his conquest of Gaul (present-day France, parts of Belgium, western Germany and northern Italy), the Roman leader found that the Gallic tribes were being helped by the Britons. Motivated by a desire to put an end to this assistance, and possibly encouraged by rumours of great wealth to be found across the water, he decided to launch an invasion. According to his *De Bello Gallico*, Caesar believed that the most civilized inhabitants lived in the maritime district that is now Kent and that most of the tribes further inland wore skins, lived on meat and milk and did not grow corn.

Caesar's first invasion of Britain occurred in 55 BC, when his army landed on an evenly sloping beach some seven miles north of Dover and, despite fierce opposition, managed to put the Britons to flight. Although he was eventually forced to abandon his foothold in Kent, Caesar returned the following year with far greater numbers, all the more determined to win a resounding victory. Landing unopposed, his army of five legions and 2,000 cavalry stormed through south-east England, crossed the Thames and successfully captured the main stronghold of the British king, Cassivellaunus. Although Caesar withdrew his legions from Britain, never to return, his expeditions proved that the main obstacle to a successful invasion was the hostility of the Channel, with its capricious weather and tides. For ninety-seven years the Romans left the island alone. When they next invaded, in AD 43 under the command of Aulus Plautius, it was in earnest. Landing at Richborough in Kent, with possibly a second landing near Chichester, the estimated 40,000-strong invasion force embarked on the start of a carefully planned campaign that would eventually end with England and Wales, and for a time southern Scotland, becoming a consular province of the mighty Roman Empire.

After the withdrawal of the legions in the early fifth century, the island gradually was conquered by Germanic tribes that had migrated across the Rhine and overrun Gaul: the Jutes mainly settled in Kent, the Saxons in Wessex, Essex and Sussex, and the Angles along the eastern coast, eventually penetrating westward into the Midlands to found Mercia. The event said to mark the beginning of English history was the landing of the Jutish mercenaries Hengest and Horsa at Ebbsfleet, near Sandwich, in AD 449. To commemorate the 1,500th anniversary of the occasion, a crew of fifty-three Danes rowed a replica dragon-headed Viking ship across the North Sea in July 1949. It now stands on the cliff top, overlooking the mud-flats of Pegwell Bay. A short distance inland is a cross commemorating the more peaceful landing, in 597, of forty monks led by St Augustine: an event that was to lead to the founding of the Church, at Canterbury, and the conversion of the Anglo-Saxons to Christianity.

Like the Romans, the Anglo-Saxons erected strongholds along the south-east coast, and by the eleventh century a number of the larger and richer ports had formed an alliance to protect their mutual interests and secure the Channel crossing. The original group, known as the Cinque Ports, consisted of Sandwich, Dover, Hythe, Romney and Hastings; two more, Winchelsea and Rye, were added after the Norman Conquest. In return for certain rights and privileges, which almost amounted to self-government, the citizens of the 'Cinque Ports and Two Ancient Towns' agreed, when called upon, to provide a royal fleet for the defence of the realm. It was not until 1278, however, that the unique privileges of the confederation as a whole were confirmed by Royal Charter. Corporate and non-corporate members, amounting to over thirty additional towns and fishing villages, joined the main seven at various times. These included Seaford, Pevensey, Lydd, Folkestone, Faversham, Fordwich and Tenterden, some of which, because of the shifting coastline, became marooned inland and ceased to be ports, while others like Deal and Walmer, which remained on the seashore, increased significantly in status.

After reaching their zenith in the mid-twelfth to mid-fourteenth centuries, the Cinque Ports gradually declined in importance. This was due to two interrelated factors: the loss of harbours, caused by the movements of shingle and silt, and the establishment of a permanent Royal Navy, begun by the Tudors. Today, despite the loss of their practical relevance, the confederation retains an important ceremonial identity which is reflected in the names of recent Lord Wardens of the Cinque Ports (once one of the most powerful and influential appointments in the realm): Sir Winston Churchill, the Australian statesman Sir Robert Menzies, and Her Majesty Queen Elizabeth The Queen Mother. The only one of the seven-strong confederation to have maintained its status as a major seaport is Dover. As the viability of the medieval harbour at the mouth of the

River Dour became increasingly threatened by cliff erosion and silting, the port was rebuilt in the area of the present docks. By constantly adapting to meet the changing needs of shipping, Dover developed into what is now the largest passenger port in the British Isles. Yet its position as the nation's third busiest point of entry, surpassed only by the airports of Heathrow and Gatwick, has come under threat from an idea first put forward in 1802 by a French mining engineer, Albert Mathieu-Favier.

Although many had dreamt of creating a fixed link between Britain and continental Europe, it was Mathieu-Favier who saw the possibility of digging a tunnel through the chalk floor of the Channel. Yet, despite interest from Napoleon, his plans never got beyond the drawing-board. Other schemes envisaged during the nineteenth century included attaching huge pipes to the sea-bed and building artificial islands linked by a chain of bridges. The notion also had its objectors. 'What!', exclaimed Lord Palmerston in 1858. 'You pretend to ask us to contribute to a work the object of which is to shorten a distance we find already too short?' In the 1870s, however, Britain and France agreed to cooperate in the construction of a tunnel. But it was not to be. After years of preparatory work and the commencement of excavations, the project was abandoned because of the perceived threat to Britain's security.

Interest in constructing a Channel tunnel was revived in the 1950s. But it was not until 1987, after much prevarication, that work began on a privately funded rail tunnel, linking a point north-east of Folkestone to another south-west of Calais. In fact, the so-called Chunnel or Eurotunnel is three tunnels: two rail tunnels, one in each direction, and a third and smaller service tunnel, with cross-links giving access to both main tunnels. Mainly following the flint-free stratum of Lower Chalk underlying the Strait of Dover, drilling took place on both sides of the Channel. Three years later, on 30 October 1990, the historic breakthrough occurred – half-way across and 128 feet below the sea-bed – when the first of the tunnels was linked by a probe-hole. Two months later, for the first time since prehistoric times, it became possible to walk on dry land between Britain and Europe. The significance of the event was not wasted by the media. 'The end of Britain's island status', proclaimed an article in the Observer Magazine of 21 November 1993, 'and the start of the first invasion of these shores since 1066.'

Pevensey Castle

In 1066, when Duke William of Normandy led his invading army ashore at Pevensey unopposed, they sheltered overnight inside the Roman fort of Anderita – one of a series of bulwarks built along the south-east coast in the third and fourth centuries as a defence against Saxon marauders. After the Conquest, William gave Pevensey to his half-brother, Count Robert of Mortain, who erected a castle within the massive walls of the fort. The keep, built in about 1100, was later strengthened by huge semicircular bastions. Although it was besieged on several occasions, including an assault by the troops of Simon de Montfort after the battle of Lewes in 1264, the castle was never taken by force. Even as a ruin, it was incorporated into England's coastal defences during the Second World War. Like many of the Cinque Ports, Pevensey (a corporate member as a limb of Hastings) lost its harbour due to silting. Today the former seaport and its castle lie over a mile inland. The Martello Towers, on the coast, were built as a defence against Napoleonic invasion.

St Thomas's Church
Winchelsea

The original settlement at Winchelsea stood on an island somewhere in the vicinity of what is now Camber Sands. One of the Two Ancient Towns of the Cinque Ports confederation, Old Winchelsea was submerged in the Great Storm of 1287. Shortly after, the present town of Winchelsea was laid out on its hill-top site in a grid plan, with a harbour at the northern end of the Iham peninsular and wharfs on the River Brede. Like Rye, Winchelsea suffered terribly from French raids during the Hundred Years' War. The church of St Thomas the Martyr was founded by Edward I at the same time as the establishment of the new town. Although conceived on an ambitious scale in the Decorated style, the church is thought not to have been completed. All that remains today are the chancel and its side chapels; the great nave and transepts were probably destroyed by the French, while the tower was demolished in 1790. As the sea withdrew and the river became narrower, Winchelsea's prosperity declined and by the end of the fifteenth century the great port was no longer.

Church Square
Rye

Standing almost three miles inland on a sandstone hill above flat, drained marshland, the historic town of Rye was originally built on a small island at the edge of the sea. During the twelfth century the town became a member of the Cinque Ports confederation under Hastings but later received full status as one of the Two Ancient Towns. After the Great Storm of 1287, which crippled or submerged such harbours as Hastings, Old Winchelsea and Romney, Rye found itself in an advantageous position, particularly as the course of the River Rother had changed to place the port at its mouth. Although the eastern part of Rye was devoured by waves in 1340, the port suffered most from attacks by the French during the fourteenth and fifteenth centuries. Despite being sacked in 1377, the medieval market town recovered much of its former prosperity, and in 1573 Elizabeth I granted it the title 'Rye Royal'. Today the sea has receded, leaving the harbour little more than a creek. Amongst the steep cobbled streets are many notable buildings including Ypres Tower and the houses around the church.

St Clement's Church
Old Romney

Standing on the site of an Anglo-Saxon foundation, the church of St Clement at Old Romney dates from the twelfth century. Restoration in 1959, which included a new stairway to the eighteenth-century minstrel's gallery, was partly funded by the Rank organization who used the church for scenes in a film about the fictional Dr Syn. When Cobbett rode through the village in September 1823, he remarked that the church was 'fit to contain one thousand five hundred people, and there are, for the people of the parish to live in, twenty-two, or twenty-three houses!' Old Romney's prosperity as one of the original Cinque Ports gradually deteriorated as a result of silting and land reclamation. At its height, the ancient port was situated on the wide estuary of the River Rother. As the sea receded, the original settlement gradually expanded eastward towards the sea and by about 1220 it was referred to as Old and New Romney. During the Great Storm of 1287 the Rother was dramatically diverted to Rye. New Romney ceased to be a port, but retained its status as 'Capital of the Marsh'.

Midley
near Lydd

All that survives of the deserted medieval village of Midley, a mile or so north-west of Lydd, is the solitary west wall of the parish church. There are several church ruins in Romney Marsh, including the more substantial, yet roofless, remains of All Saints at Hope, midway between Old and New Romney. Lydd, four miles inland from Dungeness, was once a corporate member of the Cinque Ports confederation under New Romney. The 'wool' church of All Saints, with fragments dating from Anglo-Saxon times, is 199 feet long with a tower 132 feet high. Known as the 'Cathedral of the Marsh' because of its size and splendour, All Saints stands as a reminder of the importance of Lydd in medieval times. In *The Cinque Ports*, published in 1900, Ford Madox Ford wrote that 'Lydd, if not quite the town at the end of the world, is the town next to it'. Lydd gives its name to the explosive 'lyddite', which was first tested in 1888 on the artillery ranges of the military camp to the south-west. Like Midley, Lydd was once an island in a great shallow bay that stretched from Hythe to Winchelsea and as far inland as Appledore.

Dungeness

The broad, triangular peninsula at Dungeness contains the largest continuous area of shingle in Britain. Among the plants found growing in the shingle, which forms a succession of long, rounded ridges, are clumps of sea kale, dwarf broom, thrift, yellow-horned poppy and the rare Nottingham catchfly. At Holmstone, south-west of Lydd, is a unique and ancient wood consisting almost entirely of holly. There have been five lighthouses at Dungeness. The first, erected in 1615 by Sir Edward Howard, was demolished after being stranded inland by the receding sea. All that is left of the lighthouse of 1792, built by Samuel Wyatt, is the base in which the keepers lived. The oldest of the two which stand today is 143 feet high and dates from 1904. It was replaced by a tall, slender, black-and-white lighthouse in 1961. Dominating the flat landscape are the huge reactors of two nuclear power stations, Dungeness 'A' and 'B', completed in 1965 and 1983-5 respectively. Some of the assorted bungalows on the shingle have been made from old railway carriages.

St Leonard's Church
Hythe

Standing on steep ground above Hythe, the parish church of St Leonard, dating from Norman times, is perhaps most famous for its crypt, which is stacked with some 2,000 human skulls dating from the medieval period. Lionel Lukin (1742-1834), who converted a fishing boat into the first lifeboat, is buried in the churchyard. One of the five original Cinque Ports, Hythe has its origins in the Roman fort of Lemanis, which once guarded a deep and sheltered inlet known as the Limene. As the inlet silted up, a new, Anglo-Saxon settlement sprung up to the east and was given the name Hythe, meaning a 'haven'. It was from Saltwood Castle, north of the town, that four of King Henry II's knights set out for Canterbury on 29 December 1170 to murder Archbishop Thomas Becket. The Royal Military Canal, stretching from Hythe to Winchelsea, was completed in 1806 to create a nineteen-mile-long navigable waterway and a line of defence against Napoleonic invasion. The Romney, Hythe and Dymchurch Railway opened in 1927 and runs for almost fourteen miles between Hythe and Dungeness.

Folkestone Harbour

The old fishing village of Folkestone – important enough to have been a corporate member of the Cinque Ports under Dover – began to develop as a seaside resort with the arrival of the railway from London in 1843-4. The viaduct, considered by John Newman to be 'the most exciting piece of architecture in the town', was built by William Cubitt. Today Folkestone is a major cross-Channel port, with a railway station right on the harbour. The seafront is notable for its cliff-top gardens, known as the Leas, which stretch westward for about a mile from the town centre almost to Sandgate. Within the gardens is a statue of William Harvey, the discoverer of the circulation of the blood, who was born in the town in 1578. The North Downs reach the sea east of the harbour: the town's east cliffs are therefore chalk, while those to the west are sand. At nearby Cheriton the Eurotunnel Exhibition Centre has an observation tower overlooking the Channel Tunnel terminal. On display in the Kent Battle of Britain Museum at Hawkinge are relics of aircraft that fought in the 1940 battle.

Dover Castle

At Dubris, or Dover, in the first century AD the Romans established a settlement, possibly a military base, and on the eastern cliffs above, within the massive earth ramparts of an Iron Age fort, they erected a *pharos*, or lighthouse, some 80 feet high. Remarkably, the *pharos* still survives – albeit reduced to a height of 62 feet, with the top nineteen feet having been rebuilt in the fifteenth century. Beside it stands the Anglo-Saxon church of St Mary-in-the-Castle, rebuilt in the 1860s. Both of these ancient structures stand within the walls of Dover Castle, most of which, including the keep, dates from the reign of Henry II (1154-89). Among subsequent alterations and additions are the gatehouses and 'Underground Works' of Hubert de Burgh, Constable of Dover and, from 1215, Chief Justiciar of England. In the chalk beneath the castle is a network of underground tunnels known as 'Hellfire Corner'. Veiled in official secrecy until 1986, they date from Napoleonic times and were in use during the Second World War. The entrance to the tunnels is located within the castle walls.

Bockhill Farm
St Margaret's at Cliffe

The white cliffs of Dover and South Foreland have long been a landmark for ships sailing through the English Channel. Today stretches of the famous chalk cliffline are protected by the National Trust, including Langdon Cliffs, Lighthouse Down and Kingsdown Leas. In places where the ancient grassland has survived, the cliff tops support a rich variety of flora together with butterflies like the adonis and chalk-hill blues, while the cliffs themselves are inhabited by kittiwake, fulmar and peregrine falcon. The South Foreland Lighthouse, rebuilt in 1843, is also in the care of the National Trust. In 1898 it was used by Marconi to carry out experiments in radio communications as an aid to navigation. On the cliff top, near Dover Castle, is a memorial to Louis Blériot, who accomplished the first flight across the Channel in 1909. Two further record-breaking feats are commemorated by memorials on Dover seafront: Matthew Webb's swim across the Channel in 1875 and Charles Augustus Rolls' two-way flight across the Channel in 1910.

Walmer Castle

In 1539, fearing a French invasion of England, Henry VIII ordered the building of a chain of coastal defences facing the Continent. The largest of the early castles were erected at Sandown, Walmer and Deal and were known as the 'Three Castles which keep the Downs' because they guarded the sheltered anchorage of 'The Downs', the stretch of water between the Goodwin Sands and the Kent coast. Since the early eighteenth century Walmer Castle has been the official residence of the Lords Warden of the Cinque Ports and as such has been transformed into an elegant stately home. Among those who have lived at the castle are William Pitt the Younger and the Duke of Wellington. Much of the garden was laid out by Lady Hester Stanhope while she was staying with Pitt during his office as Lord Warden in 1792-1806. Further planting was carried out by Earl Granville (Lord Warden 1865-1891). In contrast to Walmer, the castle at Deal has survived almost in its original form, and both are in the care of English Heritage. Sandown Castle, however, has been reduced by the sea to a ruin.

Barbican
Sandwich

The northern entrance to the medieval walled town and ancient Cinque Port of Sandwich is guarded by the Barbican, built in 1539 as part of Henry VIII's coastal defences against threatened invasion. During the twentieth century buildings were added to make it into a toll gate. In Anglo-Saxon times Sandwich was a thriving town and stronghold at the mouth of the River Stour. At its height, between the eleventh and thirteenth centuries, the port had a harbour at the head of the Wantsum Channel, which at that time separated the Isle of Thanet from the mainland. Today, due to the gradual silting up of the Stour (hastened by the Great Storm of 1287), the town is some two miles from the nearest sea. On the Quay, near the Barbican, is the Fisher Gate – the only one of five town gates to survive – the lower half of which is thought to date from 1384. The first bridge to cross the Stour by the Barbican was a drawbridge erected in 1759 to replace a ferry, the rights of which had been granted by King Canute in 1023 to Christ Church Abbey (later Canterbury Cathedral).

CANTERBURY AND THE WEALD OF KENT

Chiddingstone

Much of the village of Chiddingstone is owned by the National Trust, including the much-photographed row of sixteenth- and seventeenth-century buildings opposite the church, amongst which are the timber-framed post office, mentioned in a document of 1453, and the tile-hung Castle Inn, originally called Waterslip. Chiddingstone Castle, after which the inn was named, was once the home of the Streatfeild family, who made their fortune from the Wealden iron industry in the sixteenth and seventeenth centuries. It was transformed by Henry Streatfeild into a castellated mansion, or sham castle, in about 1805, and was the home of Denys Eyre Bower, an art collector and eccentric, from 1955 until his death in 1977. The castle (not owned by the National Trust) is often open to the public and houses Bower's private collections, including Japanese armour, Egyptian antiquities and relics of the Royal House of Stuart. In the park, behind the post office, is a large block of sandstone, known as the Chiding Stone, after which the village is said to take its name.

The murder of Archbishop Thomas Beckett in Canterbury Cathedral on 29 December 1170, followed by his rapid canonization, led to his shrine becoming one of medieval Europe's most popular places of pilgrimage. In *The Canterbury Tales*, a collection of narrative poems begun by Geoffrey Chaucer in about 1387, a group of thirty pilgrims set out for Canterbury from the Tabard at Southwark, London, with Harry Bailly, the innkeeper, as their guide. On the journey there and back each pilgrim is expected to tell four stories, with a free supper at the Tabard for whoever is deemed to have told the best. Although the work was never completed, the characters depicted represent a wide cross-section of medieval society: from a noble knight and French-speaking prioress to a brawny sixteen-stone miller and a cook with an ulcer on his knee.

The number of pilgrims thronging to Becket's shrine increased to such an extent that in 1220 Archbishop Stephen Langton arranged for the remains to be moved to the Trinity Chapel. Polydore Vergil, an Italian diplomat and historian, described the shrine before it was destroyed in 1538:

> The tomb of St. Thomas the martyr, Archbishop of Canterbury, exceeds all belief.
> Notwithstanding its great size, it is wholly covered with plates of pure gold; yet the gold is scarcely seen because it is covered by various precious stones, as sapphires, balasses, diamonds, rubies and emeralds; and wherever the eye turns something more beautiful than the rest is observed.

Although Becket's assassination and martyrdom has inspired numerous written works, notably T.S. Eliot's drama in verse, *Murder in the Cathedral* (1935), Canterbury's main literary association is generally considered to be Charles Dickens' semi-autobiographical novel, *David Copperfield*, published in 1849-50. Dickens moved to Kent in 1817, at the age of five, spending much of his childhood at Chatham. Indeed, many of his books dealt with locations, disguised or otherwise, in south-east England: Rochester, Broadstairs, Gravesend, Canterbury, Dover and Brighton, to name but a few. Dickens died on 9 June 1870 at Gadshill Place, near Rochester, leaving the manuscript of *The Mystery of Edwin Drood* unfinished. Although he was buried in Westminster Abbey, the novelist had conceived the idea of his body being laid to rest in 'one of the most peaceful and secluded churchyards in Kent, where wild flowers mingle with the grass, and the soft landscape around forms the fairest spot in the Garden of England.'

Jane Austen (1775-1817) often stayed with her brother, Edward, at Godmersham and Goodnestone. 'Kent is the only place for happiness!', she wrote. 'Everyone is rich there!' In September 1800 William Blake moved to a cottage at Felpham, near Bognor Regis, calling it 'the sweetest spot on earth'. Four years later, he was arrested and taken to Chichester. The *Sussex Advertiser* reported that he was tried at the Guildhall 'on a charge exhibited against him by two soldiers for having uttered seditious and treasonable expressions such as "Damn the King, damn all his subjects, damn his soldiers, they are all slaves; when Bonaparte comes it will be cut-throat for cut-throat, and the weakest must go to the wall."' Blake was found not guilty. But, despite his innocence, the verdict could easily have gone against him, especially since he had written a poem in praise of the French Revolution and had also been a friend of Thomas Paine, the writer and revolutionary.

From 1768 to 1774, while serving as an excise officer, Paine lodged at the Bull House in Lewes. It was during debating sessions, held at the White Hart inn, that he advanced such radical views as the abolition of slavery and the emancipation of women. In 1774, at the suggestion of Benjamin Franklin, Paine went to America, where he published a pamphlet entitled *Common Sense* (1776), encouraging independence for the colonies. Although his writings had enormous influence in America – *The Rights of Man* (1791-2) forming the basis of the Constitution – in England his effigy and books were systematically burnt.

Mervyn Peake (1911-68), novelist, artist and poet, lived at Burpham, near Arundel. His gravestone in the churchyard bears a line from one of his poems: 'To live at all is miracle enough'. John Cowper Powys also lived in the village, moving to Warre House (now Frith House) with his pregnant wife in 1902. In *The Four Men* (1912) Hilaire Belloc called the River Arun 'a valley of sacred water'. Many of his most personal reflections on the region appear in *The Cruise of the Nona* (1925), written after a sailing trip round the coast. Not surprisingly, his travel books include *Sussex* (1906), the county he resided in for most of his life. Charlotte Smith (1748-1806), who also lived in and wrote about Sussex, penned many successful novels, including *Emmeline* and *The Old Manor House*. In her poem *Beachy Head* she called the noble chalk headland: 'Imperial lord of the high southern coast!' John Keats visited various places throughout the South-East in 1817, including Margate, Canterbury and Hastings. His secret friendship with Isabella Jones, the 'lively Lady from Hastings', inspired several poems, including *The Eve of St Agnes* (1820).

Sheila Kaye-Smith, born in Hastings in 1887, spent all her life in Sussex, writing novels located in the South-East, including *Joanna Godden* (1921) set in the Romney Marshes. After her religious conversion to Anglo-Catholicism she wrote: 'I saw a beauty in the Sussex fields that I seemed hitherto only to have guessed at.' She was buried in 1956 in the graveyard of the church she built at Doucegrove, near Northiam.

The rich and varied literary heritage of Kent, Surrey and Sussex is without parallel in England. Among other famous names associated with the region are Christopher Marlowe (1564-93), Rudyard Kipling (1865-1936), Alfred, Lord Tennyson (1809-92), John Galsworthy (1867-1933), Virginia Woolf (1882-1941), H.G. Wells (1866-1946), William Butler Yeats (1865-1939), E.M. Forster (1879-1970), C.L. Dodgson (1832-98), and Arthur Conan Doyle (1859-1930). A.A. Milne (1882-1956) lived at Cotchford, a farmhouse near Hartfield, on the edge of Ashdown Forest, where he created his four classics for children which featured his son, Christopher Robin, and that 'silly old bear' Winnie-the-Pooh. William Cobbett (1763-1835), of *Rural Rides* fame, was born at Farnham. William Henry Hudson (1841-1922), author of *A Shepherd's Life*, lies buried at Worthing, in the same cemetery as the writer he so admired, Richard Jefferies, 'Prose Poet of England's Fields and Woodlands'. The diarist, John Evelyn (1620-1706), began and ended his life at Wotton, west of Dorking, while H.E. Bates, author of *The Darling Buds of May*, lived at Little Chart, near Ashford, from 1931 to 1974.

In the early twentieth century the area around Romney Marsh attracted writers like Joseph Conrad (1857-1924), Edith Nesbit (1858-1924), Ford Madox Ford (1873-1939) and Henry James, the American-born novelist, who lived at Lamb House, Rye, from 1898 until 1914, two years before his death. James' portrait of his adopted homeland, *English Hours*, published in 1905, features essays through 'alien eyes' that are 'ironical without being much so'. Visiting Rochester in 1877 he wrote: 'When I speak slightingly, by the way, of the outside of Rochester cathedral, I intend my faint praise in a relative sense. If we were so happy as to have this secondary pile within reach in America we should go barefoot to see it.' At Canterbury he went into the crypt of the cathedral where Becket was originally buried. 'While I stood there,' he wrote, 'a violent thunderstorm broke over the cathedral; great rumbling gusts and rain-drifts came sweeping through the open sides of the crypt and, mingling with the darkness which seemed to deepen and flash in corners and with the potent mouldy smell, made me feel as if I had descended into the very bowels of history.' A history that is very far from dead, thanks to the wealth of literary talent in the region.

Chartwell

Standing high on the slopes of the North Downs overlooking the Weald of Kent and Sussex, Chartwell is celebrated for being the home of Sir Winston Churchill from 1922 until his death in 1964. The house and surrounding eighty acres of land were given to the National Trust in 1946 on the understanding that Churchill should be allowed to live there undisturbed for his lifetime. Although the origins of the house are late medieval, when Churchill purchased the property it was essentially Victorian, and during the early 1920s it was almost completely rebuilt by Philip Tilden. The rooms today are furnished much as they were in the Churchills' time, with many of their possessions on display. In the study is the Union Jack which was unfurled in Rome on 4 June 1944 and was the first British flag to fly over a liberated European capital. It was at Chartwell that Churchill wrote many of his great works, including *A History of the English-Speaking Peoples* (1956-8). A collection of the statesman's own paintings can be seen in the garden studio.

Squerryes Court

Although built by Sir Nicholas Crisp in 1681 during the reign of Charles II, Squerryes Court at Westerham is a typical example of what came to be known as the William and Mary style. Sold to Edward Villiers, first Earl of Jersey, in 1700, it remained with the Villiers family until 1731, when it was purchased by John Warde, the ancestor of the present owners. George Warde was a close friend of James Wolfe and, shortly after the general's death at the battle of Quebec in 1759, he erected the cenotaph in the garden. The Wolfe Room contains a portrait of the soldier shortly after he received his first commission, aged fourteen, at Squerryes in 1741. Although the grounds were terraced and laid out when the red-brick house was built, much of their present appearance is due to landscaping in the eighteenth century. In more recent times the Wardes have restored part of the formal garden to the east of the house, basing their designs on a print in John Harris's *History of Kent* (1719). The River Darent rises from springs in the lake and park.

Hever Castle

On the banks of the River Eden, Hever Castle was originally built in the thirteenth century as a semi-fortified house. In 1462 the property was acquired by Sir Geoffrey Bullen and subsequently became the childhood home of Anne Bullen (or Boleyn), Henry VIII's second wife, whom he married in 1533 and beheaded, ostensibly for adultery, three years later. Hever Castle was subsequently confiscated by the Crown and eventually given to Henry's fourth wife, Anne of Cleves. After her death in 1557 it was sold to the Waldegrave family and by the end of the nineteenth century, after a succession of different owners, the castle had fallen into disrepair. The American millionaire, William Waldorf Astor, purchased the estate in 1903, and under the supervision of the architect Frank L. Pearson the castle was sympathetically restored. Outside the moat they also created a 'Tudor Village' – a linked group of cottages with over a hundred rooms in which guests could be accommodated. In the grounds are a maze, a magnificent Italian garden and a 35-acre lake.

West Entrance
Ightham Mote

A medieval, moated, courtyard house standing in a wooded valley four miles east of Sevenoaks, Ightham Mote was bequeathed to the National Trust in 1985 and its restoration involved one of the largest conservation programmes ever undertaken by the charity. Meticulous research into the house's complicated history has revealed that the first buildings – the Great Hall, the Chapel, the Crypt and the two Solars – were erected in the 1340s. This range of buildings stood at the eastern side of a moated quadrangle. The west wing was added in about 1480, with probably an entrance gate where the gatehouse tower (erected between about 1497 and 1530) now stands. By the mid-sixteenth century the quadrangle had been completely enclosed, with an open-sided gallery, or loggia, on the north side, linking the chambers of the west range with the domestic quarters of the east. Although the main fabric had been completed by 1530, further alterations and additions were carried out over the following 300 years. Nearby Knole, also owned by the Trust, is the largest private house in England.

Museum of Kent Life
Cobtree

In 1825 William Cobbett praised the ten miles between Maidstone and Tonbridge, known as the 'Garden of Eden':

> for there are not only hop-gardens and beautiful woods, but immense orchards of apples, pears, plums, cherries and filberts, and these, in many cases, with gooseberries and currants and raspberries beneath; and, all taken together, the vale is really worthy of the appellation which it bears.

The Museum of Kent Life – occupying a 26-acre site at Cobtree, near Maidstone – was established in 1985 to celebrate the rich heritage of the Kent countryside and the people who have nurtured and developed it over the centuries. Among its many attractions are historic buildings including oasthouses, demonstrations of traditional crafts, agricultural displays, livestock, special events, an exhibition of H.E. Bates and 'The Darling Buds of May', and gardens where hops, herbs, orchard fruits, vegetables and other crops are grown. The Whitbread Hop Farm at Beltring, near Paddock Wood, boasts the largest collection of Victorian oasthouses in the world.

Archbishop's Palace
Maidstone

Situated at the confluence of the rivers Medway and Len, the medieval market town of Maidstone was dominated by the Archbishops of Canterbury, who were lords of the manor from 1207 until 1537. The original manor house, which served as a country residence and a convenient resting-place on the slow and arduous journey between London and Canterbury, was rebuilt in the form of a palace in the mid-fourteenth century. Further building took place in the late fifteenth century, and during Elizabethan times the east front was added by the Astley family, who owned the property from 1581 to 1720. The palace is now a Heritage Centre, with displays illustrating the turbulent history of the building and the town. In addition to being involved in such uprisings as Wat Tyler's Peasants' Revolt of 1381, Jack Cade's rebellion of 1450 and Sir Thomas Wyatt's revolt against Mary I in 1554, Maidstone was captured by the Parliamentarians under Sir Thomas Fairfax in 1648. Today the town is the commercial and regional capital of the county.

Leeds Village

The church of St Nicholas, dating from Anglo-Saxon times, has a massive fortress-like tower of early Norman construction. It is crowned by a small spire, with dormer windows at each of the four cardinal points. Among other buildings of interest in the village, which contains many attractive cottages and half-timbered houses, are Battel Hall, dating from the early fourteenth century, and the misnamed Manor House, which was in fact the gatehouse of an Augustinian priory founded in 1119. Excavation of the foundations in 1973 revealed that the priory church was over 250 feet long. Three miles south-west of Leeds, on the edge of the escarpment overlooking the Weald, stand the ruins of Sutton Valence Castle, built in the second half of the twelfth century to protect the important medieval route that ran from Rye to Maidstone. Sutton Valence derives the latter part of its name from William de Valence, half-brother of Henry III, who was granted the castle in 1265. At Otham, west of Leeds, is Stoneacre, a half-timbered Wealden house owned by the National Trust.

Leeds Castle

Built upon two small islands in a lake, the magnificent castle at Leeds – four miles east of Maidstone – has been a Norman stronghold, the residence of six of England's medieval queens, a palace of Henry VIII and the home of three notable English families – the St Legers, the Culpepers and the Fairfaxs. A timber stronghold stood on the site beside the River Len in Anglo-Saxon times. The present stone castle dates from about 1119, when Robert de Crèvecoeur, who also founded Leeds priory, erected a keep on what is now the island support-ing the 'Gloriette'. It is thought that the defensive lake may have been created in the early or mid-thirteenth century. Royal ownership of the castle began in 1278, six years after Edward I's accession to the throne. With extensive alterations, the castle became one of the king's favourite residences. His wife, Eleanor of Castile, became the first of the six queens to hold the castle personally. The last was Catherine de Valois, widow of Henry V. Today the property belongs to the Leeds Castle Foundation and is open to the public.

Scotney Castle

In the valley of the River Bewl, near Lamberhurst, the moated remains of Scotney Castle date from the late fourteenth century when Roger Ashburnham fortified his manor house, probably as a result of the sacking of Rye and Winchelsea by French raiders in 1377. Subsequent alterations to the building included the addition of a house in about 1630 and the demolition of parts of the old castle. Between 1837 and 1843 Edward Hussey built a new house on the hill overlooking the castle, after obtaining advice from William Sawrey Gilpin, nephew of the Reverend William Gilpin, noted for his writings on the 'picturesque'. Stone for the building, designed by Anthony Salvin, was quarried from the hillside immediately below the site. Today, viewed from the house in Gilpin's 'picturesque' tradition, the shrub-filled quarry provides a dramatic foreground to the moated ruins of the old castle in the valley below. In 1977 a sculpture in bronze by Henry Moore was sited on an isthmus in the lake as a memorial to Christopher Hussey, who gave Scotney to the National Trust in 1970.

Cottage Garden
Sissinghurst

Created in the 1930s by Vita Sackville-West and her husband, Sir Harold Nicolson, the five-and-a-half-acre garden at Sissinghurst is laid out as a series of 'outdoor rooms' around the remains of a mansion erected in about 1560-70 by Sir Richard Baker. Between 1756 and 1763 the mansion was turned into a prison camp for French prisoners of war, and in about 1800 much of the building was demolished. One of the first things that the Nicolsons did when they bought the property in 1930 was to plant a white rose, 'Madame Alfred Carrière', against the wall of the cottage shown in the photograph. Some three miles east, the Wealden village of Biddenden is famous for the story of the Siamese twins, Eliza and Mary Chulkhurst, who were born in about 1100, joined together at shoulder and hip. When one of them died, at the age of thirty-four, the other refused to allow physicians to try and separate them, saying: 'We came together. We will go together.' The charity to which they bequeathed land in order to help the poor and needy of the village still exists today.

Union Mill
Cranbrook

Towering above the rooftops of the 'Capital of the Weald', the white weather-boarded Union Mill, built in 1814, is considered to be one of the finest working smock mills in England. Its name is derived from the Union of Creditors who took over the business in 1819 when the owner, Henry Dobell, went bankrupt. From 1832 until 1958 the mill belonged to the Russell family. Today, having been restored by Cranbrook Windmill Association (founded in 1982), it is regularly open to the public. The church of St Dunstan is sometimes referred to as the 'Cathedral of the Weald'. Its size and grandeur reflects the prosperity of Cranbrook as a cloth-making centre from the mid-fourteenth century until the industry's decline in the region during the late sixteenth century. In addition to lavishing their wealth on rebuilding and enlarging the church, the clothiers built many fine dwellings for themselves, including several large cloth halls. Exhibits relating to the history of the market town, including the Great Fire of 1840, are on display in the museum.

Rolvenden

In 1823, after travelling through the Wealden villages of Frant, Lamberhurst, Goudhurst and Benenden, Cobbett arrived at Rolvenden:

> These villages are not like those in the iron counties, as I call them; that is, the counties of flint and chalk. Here the houses have gardens in front of them as well as behind; and there is a good deal of show and finery about them and their gardens.

Rolvenden, standing on a ridge above Romney Marsh, is particularly noted for its wide main street lined with weather-boarded and tile-hung houses, most of which were erected after a fire in the seventeenth century. The village was once on the edge of the sea. 'A whale has been found here,' wrote Arthur Mee in 1936, 'and an old boat thought to have been wrecked in the 13th century, with the skull of a man and the skeleton of a child in it.' In the south chapel of St Mary's church, and looking more like a private room, is the Hole Park or Barham Pew, dating from 1825. Great Maytham Hall, just outside the village, was designed by Sir Edwin Lutyens and built in 1910.

Little Chart

Tradition maintains that Little Chart, in the valley of the Great Stour, was the site of England's oldest hop garden, created in 1520 (Westbere, near Canterbury, makes the same claim). The medieval church in the village was so badly bomb-damaged during the Second World War that it had to be abandoned. The present church, on a different site, dates from 1955. H.E. Bates wrote the tales of the Larkin family while he was living at nearby Little Chart Forstal (named after the large green, where cattle were penned, or 'forestalled', before going to market). Befittingly, the Yorkshire Television series, *The Darling Buds of May*, used locations in and around the area. The small ramshackle farmhouse in which the Larkins lived in 'perfick' bliss and bawdy indulgence was filmed a few miles south of Pluckley, while in the village itself properties featured included The Black Horse (Pop's local, The Hare and Hounds), the School Hall (the village hall where the gymkhana was planned) and St Nicholas's church (in which Charley and Mariette were married and the family were christened).

St Mary's Church and the Pest House
Great Chart

Dominating the village of Great Chart, west of Ashford, the church of St Mary the Virgin stands on the site of an Anglo-Saxon foundation. Although it was rebuilt in the fourteenth century, fragments survive of an earlier church of about 1080. At the corner of the churchyard is a tiny timber-framed building, variously known as the Gate House, the Priest's House or the Pest House. A notice on the side reads: 'This 15th Cent. building was restored in 1957 in memory of Lillie and Robert Bruce Ward of Godinton. It is used as Library, Museum, and for Meetings.' Godinton House, set amidst parkland to the north of the village, was the home of the Toke family who owned the estate from about 1500 until 1900. Among the memorials in the church at Great Chart is a brass to Nicholas Toke, who died in 1680 at the age of ninety-three and is reputed to be the last knight to be buried in full armour. Great Chart, Little Chart and Pluckley are on the Greensand Way – the long-distance footpath running for some 100 miles between Haselmere in Surrey and Hamstreet in Kent.

Tolhurst Farm
near Smarden

Situated in the vale of the River Beult, deep in the heart of the Kent countryside, the village of Smarden originated as a clearing in the great forest of Andreadsweald. Its prosperity as a cloth-making centre began in 1331 when a group of Flemish immigrant weavers were settled in the village by Edward III. The following year the king granted Smarden a charter to hold a weekly market and annual fair. Tradition maintains that the Smarden weaving industry began in a shed at the rear of Dragon House, built by a Flemish family in 1331. The house has a frieze of dragons carved into the beam over the first-floor window. When Elizabeth I passed through Smarden on her way from Sissinghurst to Boughton Malherbe, she was so impressed that she officially confirmed Edward's charter and made it a town. Tolhurst Farm, on the road from Pluckley, heralds the rich architectural heritage of the former market town. The church of St Michael is sometimes referred to as the 'Barn of Kent' on account of its 36-foot-wide nave, spanned by a roof without aisles for support.

Chilham

Standing on the site of an Iron Age hill-fort high above the valley of the Great Stour, some six miles south-west of Canterbury, Chilham is noted for its castle, church and village square of half-timbered houses, shops and inns. During Caesar's second invasion of Britain in 54 BC the Celts ambushed the advancing Roman legions and killed the military tribune, Quintus Laberius Durus. He is said to have been buried in the Neolithic long barrow on Juliberrie Down, on the opposite bank of the river. Although there is some doubt about whether there was a Roman fort on the chalk promontory where Chilham Castle now stands, it was certainly an Anglo-Saxon stronghold. Tradition maintains that Chilham was the home of several kings, including Vortigern, Hengest and Wihtred. The present castle consists of a Norman keep and a red-brick Jacobean mansion, built for Sir Dudley Digges between 1603 and 1616. Memorials to the Digges family can be found in the much restored St Mary's church, with its Perpendicular tower. The Pilgrims' Way and the North Downs Way (via Canterbury) pass through the village.

St Augustine's Abbey
Canterbury

After the Roman invasion of AD 43 the Iron Age settlement at Canterbury, on the banks of the Great Stour, was transformed into a fortified town and administrative capital, known as Durovernum Cantiacorum. Remains of Romano-British occupation include parts of the city wall, heightened in the Middle Ages, and the foundations of a large theatre. St Martin's, reputed to be the oldest parish church in England, may also date from Roman times. In 598 St Augustine founded a monastery outside the eastern walls of the city. It became a burial place for the early Archbishops of Canterbury, including St Augustine himself, together with Kings of Kent, such as Ethelbert and Wihtred. Alterations and additions to the original Anglo-Saxon buildings included the erection of three further churches, two of which were linked by an uncompleted rotunda started in about 1050 by Abbot Wulfric. After the Conquest the Normans built a new church on the site. The remains of the Benedictine abbey are now in the care of English Heritage.

Canterbury Cathedral

In 602, four years after founding a monastery outside the city walls at Canterbury, St Augustine refounded the church inside the walls, which, according to Bede, had 'been built by Roman Christians'. It was this church that became the cathedral and primary ecclesiastical administrative centre of England. In 1070, under Archbishop Lanfranc, work began on completely rebuilding the Anglo-Saxon cathedral-priory, mainly with stone from Caen in France. Over subsequent centuries the cathedral was considerably altered and rebuilt. After the murder of Thomas Becket in 1170 and Henry II's penance there four years later, Canterbury became an important pilgrimage centre. Between 1538 and 1541 Becket's shrine was plundered, Christ Church Priory was dissolved and the cathedral refounded under the administration of a dean and chapter. Among the many medieval buildings in the city are the Westgate (built in 1375-81), the Norman castle ruins, Greyfriars (the remains of the first Franciscan friary in England) and the Poor Priests' Hospital (rebuilt in 1373 and now a museum).

ROCHESTER AND THE NORTH KENT COAST

Cooling Castle

Surrounded by farms and marsh-land in the Hoo Peninsula, the tiny village of Cooling boasts two buildings of note: the castle and the church. In 1381, after French raiders had sailed up the Thames and demonstrated the weakness of North Kent's estuarial defences, John de Cobham was granted a licence to fortify his manor house at Cooling. On one of the gatehouse towers Cobham attached a copper replica of a legal document and seal, which, in essence, stated that it was 'made in the help of the country'. The castle was subsequently owned by Sir John Oldcastle, a prominent Lollard, who was hanged and his body burned at the stake for heresy in 1417. Built in the fourteenth century, the ragstone church of St James contains a tiny vestry, the walls of which are decorated with cockle shells. The graveyard is said to be the place where Pip first encountered the escaped convict, Magwitch, in Dickens' Great Expectations. The row of 'little stone lozenges', mentioned in the novel, are near the church porch and, although belonging to the Comport and Baker children, are known as 'Pips Graves'.

'What a study for an antiquarian!' uttered Mr Pickwick when the coach in which he was travelling reached Rochester. He applied his telescope to his eye. 'Ah! fine place,' said the stranger, 'glorious pile – frowning walls – tottering arches – dark nooks – crumbling stair-cases – Old cathedral too – earthy smell – pilgrims' feet worn away the old steps – little Saxon doors – confessionals like money-takers' boxes at theatres – queer customers those monks – Popes, and Lord Treasurers, and all sorts of old fellows, with great red faces, and broken noses, turning up every day – buff jerkins too – match-locks – Sarcophagus – fine place – old legends too – strange stories: capital;' and the stranger continued to soliloquise until they reached the Bull Inn, in the High Street, where the coach stopped.

Having spent the formative years of his life in the area around Rochester and Chatham, it is not surprising that Dickens should feature the landscape of the north Kent coast in much of his writings. Rochester, as well as appearing under its own name, is also variously referred to as Cloisterham, Dullborough, Market Town, Mudfog and Great Winglebury. Most of these pseudonyms, however, are shared with Chatham, for, as Dickens himself remarked, 'If anybody present knows to a nicety where Rochester ends and Chatham begins, it is more than I do.'

The most significant factor in the history and development of both towns has been the River Medway. In the *Pickwick Papers*, Dickens described the countryside around the river at Rochester bridge:

On either side, the banks of the Medway, covered with cornfields and pastures, with here and there a windmill, or a distant church, stretched away as far as the eye could see, presenting a rich and varied landscape, rendered more beautiful by the changing shadows which passed swiftly across it, as the thin and half-formed clouds skimmed away in the light of the morning sun.

Rising in the heart of the Weald, to the east of Crawley, the Medway debouches into the Thames Estuary at Sheerness on the Isle of Sheppey and eventually into the North Sea. On its 70-mile journey amidst the Garden of England, the river passes through Tonbridge and the county capital, Maidstone, where – to the north and south of the latter – it cuts through the chalk ranges of the North Downs.

From ancient times the Medway served as a boundary: notably to distinguish a Man of Kent, born to the east, from a Kentish Man, born to the west. Legend says that in 1066 the Men of Kent carried green boughs over their heads, making William the Conqueror think, like Macbeth, that some miraculous wood was moving towards him. As soon as they were within earshot, the branches were discarded to reveal a wall of weapons. William was offered the choice of peace or war: peace if his adversaries could retain their ancient privileges; war if they were denied. He prudently chose peace, and, thereafter, the Men of Kent became known as *invicta*, or the 'unconquered' – a word which appears on the county arms.

The 'dark flat wilderness' of the Hoo Peninsular, north of Rochester, forms the setting for the opening chapters of Dickens' *Great Expectations*. Towards nightfall Pip finds himself in the overgrown churchyard at Cooling, where he encounters the escaped convict Magwitch, who threatens to cut out his heart and liver.

Other towns and villages along the North Kent Coast associated with the author include Dartford, Gravesend, Higham, Cobham, Chalk, Sittingbourne, Margate, Ramsgate and Broadstairs. In *The Uncommercial Traveller*, published in volume form in 1861, Dickens wrote about the naval dockyard at Chatham, where over the years many great fighting ships had been built including *Revenge*, *Leviathan* and Nelson's flagship *Victory*.

> Ding, Clash, Dong, BANG, Boom, Rattle, Clash, BANG, Clink, BANG, Dong, BANG, Clatter, BANG, BANG, **BANG**! What on earth is this! This is, or soon will be, the Achilles, iron armour-plated ship. Twelve hundred men are working at her now; twelve hundred men working on stages over her sides, over her bows, over her stern, under her keel, between her decks, down in her hold, within her and without, crawling and creeping into the finest curves of her lines wherever it is possible for men to twist. Twelve hundred hammerers, measurers, caulkers, armourers, forgers, smiths, shipwrights; twelve hundred dingers, clashers, dongers, rattlers, clinkers, bangers bangers bangers!

Today, by comparison, the dockyards are silent.

In *The Mystery of Edwin Drood* Dickens returned to Rochester for his inspiration:

> A brilliant morning shines on the old city. Its antiquities and ruins are surpassingly beautiful, with a lusty ivy gleaming in the sun, and the rich trees waving in the balmy air. Changes of glorious light from moving boughs, songs of birds, scents from gardens, woods, and fields – or, rather, from the one great garden of the whole cultivated island in its yielding time – penetrate into the Cathedral, subdue its earthly odour, and preach the Resurrection and the Life.

As it happened, they were the last significant words he wrote. That morning of 8 June 1870 he was taken ill and he died the following day.

Dickens House
Broadstairs

While on a walk from Ramsgate in 1836, Charles Dickens came across Broadstairs and was so impressed by the little seaside resort that he returned the following year for the first of many visits. Although unnamed, Dickens described the town in *Our English Watering-Place* (1851):

> In truth, our watering-place itself has been left somewhat high and dry by the tide of years. Concerned as we are for its honour, we must reluctantly admit that the time when this pretty little semi-circular sweep of houses tapering off at the end of the wooden pier into a point in the sea, was a gay place, and when the lighthouse overlooking it shone at daybreak on company dispersing from public balls, is but dimly traditional now.

Dickens House (now a museum) was the home of Miss Mary Strong on whom the character Betsey Trotwood, great-aunt of David Copperfield, was based. Dickens' favourite residence was Fort House, later renamed after the novel *Bleak House*. The house, greatly enlarged in the early twentieth century, contains rooms furnished with Dickens' possessions.

St Mary's Church
Higham

The redundant church of St Mary stands on the edge of the once-malarial marshes of the Hoo Peninsula, a mile or so north of Upper Higham. Dickens, who lived at nearby Gadshill Place from 1856 until his death in 1870, knew the area well and is said to have used the village and church as the setting for the opening chapters of *Great Expectations*, importing the row of tiny gravestones from Cooling churchyard. Descriptions that correspond include the village's position, 'on the flat in-shore among the alder-trees and pollards, a mile or more from the church,' and the steeple that Pip saw when Magwitch turned him upside-down. The public house, which Pip refers to as the 'Three Jolly Bargemen' and which for the blacksmith, Joe Gargery, was 'somewhere to smoke his pipe', is said to have borne a marked similarity to The Chequers (now rebuilt) at Lower Higham. The pirate's gibbet and the prison ship no longer exist, while the 'old Battery' or bulwark, erected on the coast near Cliffe by Henry VIII in 1539, was demolished when the fort was built in 1869-70.

Rochester Castle

Situated at the point where an ancient highway crossed the River Medway, Rochester was a settlement of some importance long before the Roman conquerors erected a bridge and fortified the town. Confirming its strategic importance, the Normans built a castle within the Roman walls. The first, a motte-and-bailey fortress of timber and earth, was erected soon after 1066. It was replaced by one of the earliest stone castles in England: a fortress begun by Bishop Gundulf in about 1087-8. The castle was granted to William de Corbeil, Archbishop of Canterbury, and his successors in 1127, and work immediately began on building the massive square keep, with walls twelve feet thick and over 100 feet high. After 1215, when the castle was besieged and captured by King John, it became an important royal stronghold. Badly damaged in 1264 during the Barons' War, the castle remained a ruin until the end of the fourteenth century when it was repaired and strengthened, including the construction of the northern bastion. The remains of the castle are now in the care of English Heritage.

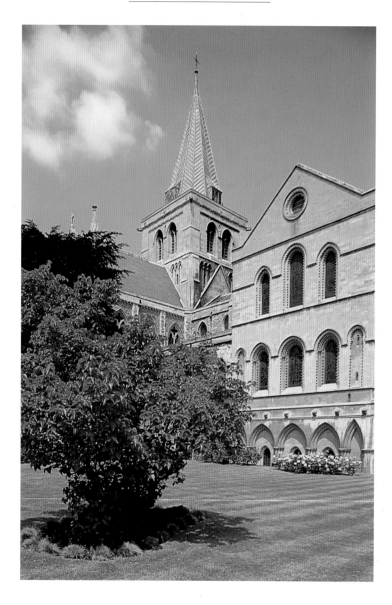

Rochester Cathedral

Standing on the site of St Andrew's church, built in 604 by Ethelbert, King of the Jutish kingdom of Kent, the cathedral-priory was founded in 1080 for Benedictine monks by Gundulf, Bishop of Rochester, who was also responsible for designing the White Tower at the Tower of London and the first stone castle at Rochester. After Gundulf's death in 1108, his successors carried on with the building of the cathedral and it was consecrated in 1130. Fires in 1137 and 1179 severely damaged the fabric, and by the end of the century the monks started to rebuild and enlarge the cathedral in the new Early English style. In 1343 the central tower and spire were erected by Bishop Hamo of Hythe. The present spire, however, dates from 1904 when the tower was being restored. St Nicholas's church, close by, was built in 1421-3 after the parishioners had been stopped by the monks from worshipping in the nave of the cathedral. Soon after the Dissolution of the Monasteries in 1540 the priory was refounded as a cathedral with a dean rather than a prior at its head.

College and Church of St Mary Magdalene
Cobham

The thirteenth-century church of St Mary Magdalene contains one of the largest collections of memorial brasses in the country, most of which depict members of the de Cobham and Brooke families, former lords of the manor. The earliest of the brasses dates from 1320 and commemorates Dame Jone de Kobeham (d. 1298). Other notable figures include Lady Joan de Cobham (d. 1433), whose fourth husband was the prominent Lollard Sir John Oldcastle, and John de Cobham (d. 1408), builder of Cooling Castle and founder of Cobham College. Standing just south of the church, the college or chantry buildings – erected in 1362 to a design by Sir Henry Yvele – were converted into almshouses by William Brooke, tenth Lord Cobham, in 1598. Brooke also built the late-Elizabethan Cobham Hall, to the east of the village, which stands in parkland laid out by Humphry Repton in about 1790. The Hall, which was the home of the Earl of Darnley, a friend of Dickens, is featured in the *Pickwick Papers*, together with the village and its 'clean and commodious' alehouse, the Leather Bottle.

Upnor Castle

During the closing years of the reign of Henry VIII (1509-47) a number of the king's ships began to use the Medway as an anchorage. The so-called 'Jillyngham Water' had two main advantages: first it was near to London, and secondly the ships could be beached on the extensive tidal mud banks for cleaning and repairs. In 1547 Henry rented a storehouse in which to keep materials and equipment. The anchorage rapidly grew in importance, and in 1550 Edward VI gave orders that all the royal ships should be harboured there. It was Elizabeth I, however, who instigated the building of the royal dockyard at Chatham from 1570 onwards. She was also responsible for building Upnor Castle, on the opposite side of the river. Work began on constructing a stone bulwark, or bastion, in 1559, which was not completed until 1567. In 1599-1601 the fort was strengthened and enlarged. After the Dutch raid of 1667, which inflicted a terrible humiliation on the English fleet, coastal defences were revised and Upnor lost its prestige as a fort to become a 'Place of Stores and Magazine'.

Arden's House
Faversham

Straddling a creek of the Swale – the tidal channel that separates the Isle of Sheppey from mainland Kent – Faversham was a flourishing Anglo-Saxon town and the site of a Cluniac (later Benedictine) abbey founded by King Stephen and Queen Matilda in about 1147. Although the 361-foot-long abbey church was demolished after the Dissolution, the gatehouse was converted into a dwelling by Thomas Arden, who became Mayor of Faversham in 1547. His murder in the house on 15 February 1550 was dramatized in *The Tragedy of Mr Arden of Feversham*, published in 1592. The author, who some claim was Shakespeare, remains anonymous, but the play is known to have been based on an account of the murder in Raphael Holinshed's *Chronicle* of 1587. Apparently the plot, involving Arden's wife Alice and her lover Thomas Morsby, was hatched in the fifteenth-century inn which now houses the Fleur de Lis Heritage Centre. Faversham was an important centre for gunpowder-making, and the Chart Gunpowder Mills (now restored) supplied powder to Nelson at Trafalgar and Wellington at Waterloo.

The 'Two Sisters'
Reculver

Built on the site of a monastery founded in 669 by Egbert, King of Kent, the twin towers of Reculver's ruined church of St Mary are a prominent landmark on the ten-mile stretch of coast between Margate and Herne Bay. The towers, 63 feet high, stand within the sea-eroded remains of the Roman fort of Regulbium, which guarded the northern end of the mile-wide Wantsum Channel. According to legend, in the late twelfth century the prioress of the Benedictine monastery at Davington, near Faversham, accompanied by her twin sister, set out by sea to visit the shrine of the Virgin at Broadstairs. Their boat was wrecked in a storm off Reculver and the sister died. In order to provide a lasting memorial to her memory and also a warning to mariners, the prioress erected the two western towers of St Mary's, basing their design on those at Davington church. In 1809, under threat of being washed away by the rapid encroachment of the sea, the church was demolished. The 'Two Sisters', however, were saved as an aid to navigation by Trinity House.

Botany Bay
near Margate

The sandy bays of the Thanet coast were a favourite landing-site for smugglers, who gained access to the beaches through gaps in the cliffs and stored their contraband in natural caves, hidden by bushes. In places the gangs tunnelled into the chalk to create a network of secret passages, some as long as 300 yards. In 1769 Joss Snelling and his gang were unloading a cargo at Botany Bay, between Foreness Point and Kingsgate, when they were surprised by preventative officers. In the ensuing fight, known as the 'Battle of Botany Bay', fifteen smugglers lost their lives: nine were fatally wounded and six were later hanged. Snelling, after whom Joss Bay is reputed to be named, avoided capture and managed to reach the ripe old age of ninety-six before he died in 1837. King Vortigern's Cavern and the Grotto, both underground caves at Margate, were rediscovered in 1798 and 1835, respectively. The cavern is thought to date from Anglo-Saxon times, while the origin of the grotto, decorated from floor to ceiling by shell designs, is a mystery.

Smock Mill
Sarre

Sarre Mill, built in 1820 and restored in 1991, is one of the few remaining, commercially worked smock mills in the country. The inland village of Sarre, or the 'Ville de Sarre' as it has long been known, stands at the western boundary of the Isle of Thanet and once operated a ferry service across the Wantsum Channel. During Roman times it was a port connected to St Lawrence, near Ramsgate, by a metalled road. Evidence that Sarre was the site of an important Anglo-Saxon cemetery, with over 250 graves, was confirmed by the archaeologist John Brent in 1863 after a labourer had unearthed artifacts while digging a trench near the windmill. Among the finds, which included weapons, coins, dice and jewellery, was a unique six-inch plane of Roman design. Although the village no longer has a church, there are two public houses: the Kings Head, created in the 1790s out of two adjoining cottages, and the Crown Inn, dating from 1492 and nicknamed the 'Cherry Brandy House' because of a unique brew of cherry brandy introduced by the landlord in 1685.

Minster Abbey

The parish church of St Mary (near the abbey) at Minster-in-Thanet stands on the site of a nunnery founded in about 670 by Ermenburga, later St Domneva, a princess of Kent and the mother of three saints: Milburga, Mildred and Mildgyth. Ermenburga the first abbess, was succeeded by Mildred, whose piety and goodness attracted many nuns to the monastery. In order to cope with the increased numbers, the third abbess, Edburga, founded a new and larger nunnery on the site of the present abbey. During the ninth century the nunnery's prosperity declined dramatically because of raids by Danish pirates and in about 840 it was destroyed. The land, which reverted to the Crown, was granted to St Augustine's Abbey, Canterbury, by King Canute in 1027. The monks built St Mary's church and restored the remains of the nunnery for use as the grange, or administrative headquarters, of their extensive manor of Minster. The farm buildings, dating from about 1027, only became an abbey in 1937 when they were purchased by a community of Benedictine nuns from Germany.

Lighthouse
North Foreland

In a letter to Professor Felton, dated 1843, Dickens called the North Foreland lighthouse 'a severe parsonic light, which reproves the young and giddy floaters, and stares grimly out upon the sea'. Standing on high chalk cliffs, a mile or so north of Broadstairs and at the eastern-most point of Kent, the present lighthouse was built in the late seventeenth century to warn shipping of the treacherous Goodwin Sands, seven miles off-shore. Eighty-five feet high, the light has a powerful beam that is visible for over twenty miles. In 1683, on their way by sea from London to Dover, Charles II and his brother (later James II) put in for shelter at one of the bays to the north, and to commemorate the event a gate was erected. The bay, known as St Bartholomew's after an earth tremor on the day of the saint had opened a fissure in the cliffs, was renamed Kingsgate. Among the follies erected at Kingsgate by Lord Holland from the 1760s onwards, but later much altered, are Port Regis, Kingsgate Castle and the Captain Digby inn.

Ramsgate Harbour

In 1586 the historian William Camden praised the inhabitants of Ramsgate, Margate and Broadstairs:

> For they are exceeding industrious, are as it were Amphibious creatures, and get their living both by sea and land; they deal in both elements, are both fishers and ploughmen, both husbandmen and mariners; and the selfsame hand that holds the plough, steers the ship likewise.

Ramsgate, by then, was a non-corporate member of the Cinque Ports under Sandwich. Situated in a gap, or gate, between two gently sloping cliffs of chalk, the natural haven was sheltered by a jetty projecting out from the headland. From 1688 the town began to prosper through trade with Baltic ports, and in 1749 work began on the construction of a harbour, which was not completed until after the erection of the lighthouse in 1791. From a busy fishing and trading port Ramsgate developed into a fashionable Regency sea-bathing resort with elegant terraces on both east and west cliffs. In June 1940, during the Second World War, the 'Royal Harbour' played a vital role in the evacuation of Dunkirk.

Richborough Castle

After landing unopposed on British soil in AD 43 the Roman army, under Aulus Plautius, quickly established a bridgehead fort at Richborough and from there they launched their successful invasion of the island. The site soon became an important military and naval supply base with roads running west to Durovernum (Canterbury) and south to Dubris (Dover). Soon after AD 85, the Romans confirmed Richborough's status as the gateway to the provinces of imperial Britain by constructing a huge triumphal arch, estimated to be 80 feet high, 88 feet wide and 48 feet deep, of which only the foundations now remain. By the second century Rutupiae (Richborough) had developed into a prosperous town and cross-Channel port, with a natural harbour at the southern end of the tidal Wantsum Channel, which, before it was blocked by silting, was between one and three miles wide. The long stretches of stone walls that survive at Richborough today date from about AD 285, when the Romans built a massive fort to defend the coast against Saxon sea-raiders.

St Augustine's Cross
Ebbsfleet

Erected in 1884 by Earl Granville, Lord Warden of the Cinque Ports, St Augustine's Cross bears a plaque which reads:

> After many dangers and difficulties by land and by sea Augustine landed at last on the shores of Richborough in the Isle of Thanet. On this spot he met King Ethelbert and preached his first sermon to our countrymen. Thus he happily planted the Christian faith which spread with marvellous speed throughout the whole of England.

Augustine's landing at Ebbsfleet in 597 is one of two historic landings to be commemorated in the locality. On the cliff top overlooking Pegwell Bay stands the replica of a dragon-headed Viking ship which was rowed across the North Sea from Esbjerg, Denmark, in 1949, to mark the 1,500th anniversary of Hengest and Horsa's landing at Ebbsfleet. After their arrival the crew of fifty-three Danes 're-enacted the meeting of their ancestors with King Vortigern of Kent and his subsequent betrothal to Hengest's daughter Rowena'. Built of Danish oak secured by copper nails, the longship is 71 feet in length.

PHOTOGRAPHER'S NOTES

Cuckmere River
from Exceat

At the western edge of Friston Forest, near Westdean and Exceat, the Cuckmere River makes a series of dramatic meanders before entering the Channel at Cuckmere Haven. Although water follows the bends, the main river takes a more direct route to the sea by way of a straight, artificial channel cut in 1846. Unlike other Sussex rivers, the Cuckmere never possessed a port at its mouth, although in earlier times it was navigable as far as Alfriston. Exceat was a small fishing village until the number of inhabitants declined because of the Black Death in 1348 and repeated incursions by French sea raiders. It became part of the parish of Westdean in 1528, and all that now remains is a farm and the foundations of the church, excavated in 1913. When smuggling was at its height along the south-east coast, Cuckmere Haven, with its flat, pebble beach, was a popular spot for landing illegal goods. A letter dated 1783 mentions an occasion when 200-300 smugglers on horseback 'received various kinds of goods from the boats ... in defiance of the Kings' officers'.

Basically, the equipment I use falls into two categories: a 35mm Nikon with a wide range of lenses, 24mm, 28mm, 35mm, 85mm and 180mm; and a medium-format Hasselblad with, on most occasions, just three lenses, 50mm, 80mm and 150mm. The Hasselblad is used essentially for landscapes. The Nikon was purchased new some twelve years ago, while all the lenses were obtained second hand. With its missing knobs and buttons, numerous dents and scratched paintwork, the camera may look a little sad, but it has proved to be totally reliable. I turned to using the Hasselblad system at the beginning of this book, when I could stand the frustrations of camera breakdown in two out of my three previous kits no longer. If the clockwork Hasselblad stands up to professional use like the Nikon, I'll be well pleased. All my equipment is carried in quality back-packs (the type designed for walkers) which cost a lot less than camera bags and provide adjustable weight distribution between hips and shoulders. I use a Linhof tripod which, despite being large and very stable, is surprisingly lightweight. In addition to a hand-held light meter (with which I always measure the light falling onto the subject not that reflected from it), I carry numerous other accessories such as filters and a compass.

As most books on improving camera technique will reveal, photography is about identifying potentially good subjects and using composition and light to the best effect, about anticipation and preparation so that when all is at its best you can, hopefully, be there with the shutter open. Creature comforts also play their part. Wearing comfortable and adequate clothing and having a supply of food and drink all help the mind to remain focused on the job, which must surely lead to better pictures. But one accessory that I could never do without is my photographic assistant, George. Remarkably, he takes everything in his stride. His is a no-nonsense approach to photography. Blessed with infinite, never-complaining patience, George shows no interest in camera equipment. His prime objective is to get the job over as quickly as possible so that he can claim his reward: a bit of fuss and a well-earned biscuit. George, a Border Collie, has accompanied me on every assignment for the last five years. So far, he's proved trustier than any camera, even my bashed, but ever-enduring Nikon.

Rob Talbot

SELECTED PROPERTIES AND REGIONAL OFFICES

ENGLISH HERITAGE

All English Heritage properties, except where specified, are open from April to the end of October every day from 10am to 6pm (summer season); from November to March opening times are Tuesdays to Sundays from 10am to 4pm. The properties are closed on 24–26 and 1 January. Opening hours are subject to change so please contact properties before making your journey.

Customer Services Department,
PO Box 569, Swindon SN2 2YP
Tel: (0870) 3331181

Historic Properties South-East
Eastgate Court, 195–205 High Street,
Guildford GU1 3EH
Tel: (01483) 252000

Battle Abbey
High Street, Battle, East Sussex TN33 0AD
Tel: (01424) 773792
Open all year; closed 25 December and 1 January.

Bayham Abbey
Lamberhurst, East Sussex TN3 8BE
Tel: (01892) 890381
March to October, open daily; November to March, weekends only.

Deal Castle
Victoria Road, Deal, Kent CT14 7BA
Tel: (01304) 372762
Open daily throughout year; closed 25–26 December and 1 January.

Dover Castle
Dover, Kent CT16 1HU
Tel: (01304) 201628 (information only)
(01304) 211067 (main office)
Open daily throughout year; closed 24–26 December and 1 January.

Pevensey Castle
Pevensey, East Sussex BN24 5LE
Tel: (01323) 762604
Open April to end October daily; November to end of March, Wednesdays to Sundays; closed 24–26 December and 1 January.

Richborough Castle
Richborough, Sandwich, Kent CT13 9JW
Tel: (01304) 612013
Open daily April to end October; November to March, weekends only.

Rochester Castle
The Keep, Rochester, Kent ME1 1SW
Tel: (01634) 402276
Open daily throughout year; closed 24–26 December.

St Augustine's Abbey
Longport, Canterbury, Kent CT1 1TF
Tel: (01227) 767345
Open daily throughout year; closed 24–26 December and 1 January.

Upnor Castle
High Street, Upper Upnor, Rochester-upon-Medway, Kent ME2 4XG
Tel: (01634) 718742
Open daily April to October.

Walmer Castle and Gardens
Walmer, near Deal, Kent CT14 7LJ
Tel: (01304) 364288
Open daily April to end October; November to end December and March, Wednesdays to Sundays; January and February, weekends only; closed 24–26 December and when Lord Warden is in residence.

NATIONAL TRUST

Southern Regional Office
Polesden Lacey. Dorking,
Surrey RH5 6BD
Tel: (01372) 453401

Alfriston Clergy House
The Tye, Alfriston, Polegate,
East Sussex BN26 5TL
Tel: (01323) 870001
Open daily April to end October, except Tuesdays and Fridays.

Bateman's
Burwash, Etchingham, East Sussex TN19 7DS
Tel: (01435) 882302
Open April to end October, Saturdays to Wednesdays and Good Fridays.

Bodiam Castle
Bodiam, near Robertsbridge,
East Sussex TN32 5UA
Tel: (01580) 830436
Open daily mid-February to end October; November to January, weekends only; closed 24–26 December

Chartwell
Westerham, Kent TN16 1PS
Tel: (01732) 866368
Open March to June and September to November, Wednesday to Sunday; July and August, Tuesday to Sunday.

Clandon Park
West Clandon, Guildford, Surrey GU4 7RQ
Tel: (01483) 222482
Open daily April to end October, except Monday, Friday and Saturday; open Bank Holidays.

Claremont Landscape Garden
Portsmouth Road, Esher, Surrey KT10 9JG
Tel: (01372) 467806
Open April to end October daily; November to March, Tuesdays to Sundays; closed 25 December and 1 January.

Hatchlands Park
East Clandon, Guildford, Surrey GU4 7RT
Tel: (01483) 222482
Open early April to end October, Tuesdays to Thursdays, Sundays and Bank Holiday Mondays (and Fridays in August).

Ightham Mote
Ivy Hatch, Sevenoaks, Kent TN15 0NT
Tel: (01732) 810378
Open April to end October, Mondays, Wednesdays to Fridays, and Sundays.

Knole
Sevenoaks, Kent TN15 0RP
Tel: (01732) 462100
House open April to end October, Wednesdays to Sunday and Bank Holiday Mondays; park open daily; garden, May to September, first Wednesday in each month.

Nymans Garden
Handcross, near Haywards Heath, West Sussex RH17 6EB
Tel: (01444) 400321
Open March to end October, Wednesdays to Sundays and Bank Holiday Mondays.

Polesden Lacey
near Dorking, Surrey RH5 6BD
Tel: (01372) 452048
General NT enquiries (01372) 453401
House open April to end October, Wednesdays to Sundays and Bank Holiday Mondays; garden, open daily throughout year

Scotney Castle Garden
Lamberhurst, Tunbridge Wells, Kent TN3 8JN
Tel; (01892) 891081
Garden open April to end October, Wednesdays to Sundays and Bank Holiday Mondays; closed Good Fridays; old castle as gardens, May to mid-September.

Sheffield Park Garden
Sheffield Park, Uckfield, East Sussex TN22 3QX
Tel: (01825) 790231
Open daily March to December, except Mondays; January and February, weekends only.

Sissinghurst Garden
Sissinghurst, near Cranbrook, Kent TN17 2AB
Tel: (01580) 710700
Open daily April to November, except Wednesdays and Thursdays.

Standen
East Grinstead, West Sussex RH19 4NE
Tel: (01342) 323029
Open daily April to end October, except Mondays and Tuesdays.

Wakehurst Place
Ardingly, near Haywards Heath,
West Sussex RH17 6TN
Tel: (01444) 894066
Open daily throughout year, closed 25 December and 1 January.

Winkworth Arboretum
Hascombe Road, Godalming,
Surrey GU8 4AD
Tel: (01483) 208477
Open daily throughout year.

MISCELLANEOUS

Anne of Cleves House Museum
52 Southover High Street, Lewes,
East Sussex BN7 1JA
Tel: (01273) 474610
Open April to end October, Tuesday to Saturdays.

Archbishop's Palace and Heritage Centre
Palace Gardens, Mill Street, Maidstone,
Kent ME15 6YE
Tel: (01622) 752891
Open daily throughout year, closed 25–26 December.

Arundel Castle
Arundel, West Sussex BN18 9AB
Tel: (01903) 883136
Open April to end October, Sundays to Fridays.

Bignor Roman Villa
Bignor, Pulborough, West Sussex RH20 1PH
Tel: (01798) 869259
Open March to end October, Tuesdays to Sundays and Bank Holiday Mondays.

Charleston Farmhouse
near Firle, Lewes, East Sussex BN8 6LL
Tel: (01323) 811265
Open April to end October, Wednesdays to Sunday and Bank Holiday Mondays.

Chatham Historic Dockyard
Chatham, Kent ME4 4TE
Tel: (01634) 812551
Open daily Easter to end October; February, March and November, Wednesdays and weekends.

Chiddingstone Castle
Chiddingstone, near Edenbridge, Kent TN8 7AD
Tel: (01892) 870347
Open April and May, Easter and Bank Holidays; June to September: Wednesday to Friday, Sundays and Bank Holidays.

Firle Place
Firle, near Lewes, East Sussex BN8 6LP
Tel: (01273) 858335
Open June to end September, Wednesdays, Thursdays, Sundays and Bank Holiday Mondays.

Fishbourne Roman Palace and Museum
Salthill Road, Fishbourne, near Chichester,
West Sussex PO19 3QR
Tel: (01243) 785859
Open daily throughout year.

Glynde Place
Glynde, near Lewes, East Sussex BN8 6XX
Tel: (01273) 858224
Open May Sundays and Bank Holiday afternoons; June to September, Wednesday, Sunday and Bank Holiday afternoons.

Great Dixter House and Gardens
Northiam, near Rye, East Sussex TN13 6PH
Tel: (01797) 252878
Open April to end October, Tuesdays to Sundays and Bank Holiday Mondays.

Hever Castle and Gardens
Hever, near Edenbridge, Kent TN8 7NG
Tel: (01732) 865224
Open daily March to end November.

Leeds Castle
Maidstone, Kent ME17 1PL
Tel: (01622) 765400
Open daily throughout year; closed 25 December and on special events.

Leonardslee Gardens
Lower Breeding, near Horsham,
West Sussex RH13 6PP
Tel: (01403) 891212
Open daily April to end October.

Lewes Castle
Barbican House, Lewes, East Sussex BN7 1YE
Tel: (01273) 486290
Open daily throughout year; closed 25–26 December.

Michelham Priory
Upper Dicker, Hailsham, East Sussex BN27 3QS
Tel: (01323) 844224
Open daily end March to end October, March and November, Sundays only.

Museum of Kent Life
Lock Lane, Sandling, Maidstone,
Kent ME14 3AU
Tel: (01622) 763936
Open daily February to early November.

Priest House
West Hoathly, near East Grinstead,
East Sussex RH19 4PP
Tel: (01342) 810479
Open daily March to end October.

Penshurst Place and Gardens
Penshurst, Tonbridge, Kent TN11 8DG
Tel: (01892) 870307
Open daily end March to beginning November.

The RHS Garden, Wisley
Wisley, Woking, Surrey GU23 6QB
Tel: (01483) 224234
Open daily all year, closed 25 December.

Royal Pavilion
Old Steine, Brighton, East Sussex BN1 1EE
Tel: (01273) 290900
Open daily throughout year, closed 25–26 December

St Mary's House
Bramber, West Sussex BN44 3WE
Tel: (01903) 816205
Open Easter to end September, Sundays, Thursdays and Bank Holiday Mondays.

Squerryes Court
Westerham, Kent TN16 1SJ
Tel: (01959) 562345/563118
Open April to end September, Wednesdays, Saturdays, Sundays and Bank Holiday Mondays.

Weald and Downland Open Air Museum
Singleton, Chichester, West Sussex PO18 0EU
Tel: (01243) 811363
Open daily throughout year but only Wednesdays, Saturdays and Sundays between November and February.

Whitbread Hop Farm
Beltring, Paddock Wood, Kent TN12 6PY
Tel: (01622) 872068
Open daily throughout year, closed 24–26 December.

SELECT BIBLIOGRAPHY

Arscott, David, *Curiosities of East Sussex*, S.B. Publications, Market Drayton, 1991

Arscott, David, *Curiosities of West Sussex*, S.B. Publications, Market Drayton, 1993

Beckett, Arthur, *The Wonderful Weald*, Methuen London, revised 1924 (first pub. Mills & Boon, 1911)

Bede, The Venerable, *The Ecclesiastical History of the English Nation*, Dent, London, n.d.

Bird, Eric, and James, Lilian, *Writers on the Coast*, Windrush Press, Moreton-in-Marsh, 1992

Bray, William, (ed.), *The Diary of John Evelyn* (2 Vols.), Dent, London, n.d.

Brentnall, Margaret, *The Cinque Ports and Romney Marsh*, Gifford, London, 1972

Brooks, Sister Beda, *Saint Domneva and the Foundation of Minster-in-Thanet*, Minster Abbey Trustees, 1991

Brunnarius, Martin, *The Windmills of Sussex*, Phillimore, Chichester, 1979

Chaucer, Geoffrey, *The Canterbury Tales*, (trans. Nevill Coghill) Penguin Books, Harmondsworth, 1951

Christian, Garth, *Ashdown Forest*, Society of Friends of Ashdown Forest, Forest Row, 1967

Clifton-Taylor, Alec, *Chichester*, The Alastair Press, Bury St Edmunds, 1989

Clifton-Taylor, Alec, *Another Six English Towns*, BBC, London, 1984

Cobbett, William, *Rural Rides*, Penguin Books, Harmondsworth, 1967

Crocker, Glenys, *A Guide to the Industrial Archaeology of Surrey*, Association for Industrial Archaeology, Telford, 1990

Dale, Herbert D.,*The Ancient Town of Hythe and St Leonard's Church*, Kipps Bookshop, Hythe, 1931

Defoe, Daniel, *A Tour Thro' the Whole Island of Great Britain* (2 Vols.), Davies, London, 1927

Dyer, James, *Southern England: An Archaeological Guide*, Faber & Faber, London, 1973

Fiddes, Angela, *Brighton*, Pevensey Press, Newton Abbot, 1987

Fortey, Richard, *The Hidden Landscape*, Jonathan Cape, London, 1993

Garmonsway, G.N. (trans.), *The Anglo-Saxon Chronicle*, Dent, London, 1953

Gilpin, William, *Three Essays on Picturesque Beauty; on Picturesque Travel; and on Sketching Landscape*, Blamire, London, 1794

Hammond, J.W., (ed.), *Ward Lock's Red Guide: Eastbourne and the East-Sussex Coast*, Ward Lock, London, 1967

Hammond, J.W., (ed.), *Ward Lock's Red Guide: The Kent Coast*, Ward Lock, London, 1968

Hardwick, Michael and Mollie, *Dickens's England*, Dent, London, 1970

Hemming, Peter, *Windmills in Sussex*, C.W. Daniel, London, 1936

Herbstein, Denis, *The North Downs Way*, H.M.S.O., London, 1982

Hillier, Caroline, *The Bulwark Shore*, Granada, London, 1982

Hudson, W.H., *A Shepherd's Life*, Methuen, London, 1910

Hufton, Geoffrey, and Baird, Elaine, *The Scarecrow's Legion*, Rochester Press, Sittingbourne, 1983

Hughes, Pennethorne, *Kent*, Faber & Faber, London, 1969

Hunt, Donald, *The Tunnel: The Story of the Channel Tunnel 1802-1994*, Images, Upton-upon-Severn, 1994

James, Henry, *English Hours*, O.U.P., Oxford, 1981

Jerrold, Walter, *Highways & Byways in Kent*, Macmillan, London, 1926

Jessup, Ronald, *South-East England*, Thames and Hudson, London, 1970

Kaye-Smith, Sheila, *Weald of Kent and Sussex*, Hale, London, 1953

Leland, John, *The Itinerary of John Leland: Vol 4* (ed. Lucy Toulmin Smith), S. Illinois University, Carbondale, USA, 1964

Lloyd, Nathaniel, *A History of the English House*, Architectural Press, London, 1975 (first pub. 1931)

MacDougall, Philip, *The Hoo Peninsula*, Hallewell, Rochester, 1980

Marples, Morris, *White Horses and Other Hill Figures*, Sutton, Stroud, 1981

Massingham, H.J., *English Downland*, Batsford, London, 1936

Mathews, Oliver, *Cinque Ports*, Town & Country, Shepperton, 1984

Mee, Arthur (ed.), *Kent* (King's England series) Hodder and Stoughton, London, 1936

Mee, Arthur (ed.), *Surrey* (King's England series) Hodder and Stoughton, London, 1938

Mee, Arthur (ed.), *Sussex* (King's England series) Hodder and Stoughton, London, 1937

Morgan, Philip (ed.), *Domesday Book: Kent*, Phillimore, Chichester, 1983

Morris, John (ed.), *Domesday Book: Surrey*, Phillimore, Chichester, 1975

Morris, John (ed.), *Domesday Book: Sussex*, Phillimore, Chichester, 1976

Murray, J.C., *Romney Marsh*, Hale, London, 1953

Nairn, Ian, and Pevsner, Nikolaus, *Surrey* (Buildings of England series), Penguin Books, Harmondsworth, 1962

Nairn, Ian, and Pevsner, Nikolaus, *Sussex* (Buildings of England series), Penguin Books, Harmondsworth, 1965

Newman, John, *North East and East Kent* (The Buildings of England series), Penguin Books, Harmondsworth, 1969

Newman, John, *West Kent and the Weald* (The Buildings of England series), Penguin Books, Harmondsworth, 1969

Parker, Eric, *Surrey* (County Books series), Hale, London, n.d.

Pitt, Derek, & Shaw, Michael, *Surrey Villages*, Hale, London, 1971

Platt, Richard, *The Ordnance Survey Guide to Smugglers' Britain*, Cassell, London, 1991

Quiney, Anthony, *English Domestic Architecture: Kent Houses*, Antique Collectors Club, Woodbridge, 1993

Seymour, John, *The Companion Guide to the Coast of South East England*, Collins, London, 1975

Smith, Bernard, & Haas, Peter, *Writers in Sussex*, Redcliffe, Bristol, 1985

Spence, Keith, *The Companion Guide to Kent & Sussex*, Collins, London, 1973

Steers, J.A., *The Coastline of England and Wales*, Cambridge University Press, Cambridge, 1969

Thompson, W. Harding, and Clark, Geoffrey, *The Sussex Landscape*, Black, London, 1935

Vigar, John E., *Kent Curiosities*, Dovecote Press, Wimborne, 1992

Webb, William, *Kent's Historic Buildings*, Hale, London, 1977

White, John Talbot, *The South-East Down and Weald: Kent, Surrey and Sussex* (Regions of Britain series), Eyre Methuen, London, 1977

Winbolt, S.E., *Kent*, Bell, London, 1930

Winbolt, S.E., *Kent, Sussex & Surrey*, Penguin Books, Harmondsworth, 1939

INDEX